He Restores My Soul

Edited by Katie Schuermann

Emmanuel Press ✠ Fort Wayne, IN

For all the people of His pasture

࠮

TABLE OF CONTENTS

1. All We like Sheep — Katie Schuermann 1

2. Fight the Good Fight — Rebecca Mayes.................................9

3. What Shall I Render to the Lord? — Christina Roberts......... 21

4. Motherhood and Mental Illness — Cheryl Swope.................. 33

5. I Am Herod — Katie Schuermann.......................................43

6. Getting Past Your Past — Cheryl Magness 53

7. Incompatible with Life — Magdalena Schultz...................... 63

8. When God Is Hiding — Heidi Sias 73

9. Spare the Rod — Kristin Wassilak 83

10. Living the Creed — Mollie Hemingway 95

11. O Bride of Christ, Rejoice — Heather Smith 103

12. Torn in Two — Julia Habrecht 113

13. I Remember You — Pamela Boehle-Silva 121

14. Train Up a Child — Cheryl Swope 129

A Pastoral Response — D. Richard Stuckwisch 139

Discussion Questions 149

About the Authors.. 157

About the Artist 167

About Emmanuel Press 169

Acknowledgments 171

The LORD is my shepherd; I shall not want.
He makes me lie down in green pastures.
He leads me beside still waters.
He restores my soul.
He leads me in paths of righteousness
for His name's sake.

Even though I walk through the valley
of the shadow of death,
I will fear no evil, for You are with me;
Your rod and Your staff,
they comfort me.

You prepare a table before me
in the presence of my enemies;
You anoint my head with oil; my cup overflows.
Surely goodness and mercy shall follow me
all the days of my life,
and I shall dwell in the house
of the LORD forever.

℘

Psalm 23

CHAPTER ONE

All We like Sheep
by Katie Schuermann

"The Lord is my shepherd."
Psalm 23:1

I am a sheep prone to wander.

I feel the urge most when I plop myself down on a cushy, velvety pew—that green pasture to which the Good Shepherd has led me. I sit there safe and fat and satiated in the house of the Lord, wanting for nothing in this life, resting in the cool shade of the mountain of His promises kept for me, but my dumb, ungrateful heart bleats for the thing it does not have, the thing it thinks it deserves, the thing that has never been promised to any of us in the flock: health, happiness, honor, money, power, beauty, freedom from persecution, a soulmate, physical satisfaction, or, in my particular case, children.

I sit on that pew, fat but childless, and I begin to despise the Good Shepherd who has made me barren. Never mind the still waters. Never mind the table set with His own body. Never mind the cup overflowing with His own blood. Never mind the goodness and mercy that are mine for His name's sake. I remember only the thing I have not been given, and I scorn the Good Shepherd's bounty, turning my tail on His rod and staff.

Self-pity is self-destructive that way. It fills our hearts and minds and bellies with a yearning so loud it drowns out the

Shepherd's voice. We can no longer discern His goodness from our guts, His promises from our projections, His will from our wishes. We look upon His daily bread, now turned bland and dry on our tongues, and hunger after cake that is not of this pasture. With idiotic rapture, we wander toward our yearnings, if not with our feet, then with our hearts.

Just this last year, I wandered straight off the path of righteousness and into a thicket.

I cannot tell you the exact moment of my straying. It was a slow veer, a steady rove. I simply remember waking one morning and feeling a small, cold sun of horror dawning in my heart. It returned the next day and the next, growing hard like plaque in my arteries, blocking my peace, my joy, and my trust in the Lord.

I was traveling a lot. My husband encouraged it. We had recognized years before that our children lived outside of our home rather than in it, so I drove and flew and journeyed to them as time and opportunity allowed. Many of my children I was meeting for the first time—daughters, mothers, grandmothers, aunts, organists, artists, teachers, college students, pastors' wives, widows—blessings from God, every one of them. My empty arms grew warm with the weight of their concerns, joys, terrors, laughter, and sorrows. I felt purposeful, useful, and needed by these children beyond my front door. I felt like a mother, perhaps for the first time in my life.

But I never quite recovered from my travels. Each trip left me feeling less and less like myself. I would wake up in the middle of the night and not recognize my feelings, my thoughts, my experiences. Everything was so much, so fast. I was meeting more people than I could remember, and my recollections of them magnified in the long, dark hours of the night. I thought on those people more and more and on our Lord less and less. I grew distracted, often forgoing the still waters of God's Word to take long draughts from the strong drink of human conversation. I grew loose in my piety and strong in my psychology, tuning the dial on my personal antennae to the point of receiving every signal from every person I encountered. In my push to be a mother to everyone, I forgot to be a child of God.

A counselor labeled it compassion fatigue. I think she was right, but there was so much more going on than I ever had time to tell her. I was hitting middle age. My body was changing. My feet were falling apart from running through airports in sandals and standing in flats at a podium for hours on end. My husband was trying to find true north in the disorienting world that is pastoral ministry, and we both struggled against the age-old temptation to trust in something other than God's Word to strengthen His Church. Together we were attempting another run at foster parent certification. We were doing more and sleeping less. We stood at the kitchen counter to eat and piled the dining table with to-do lists and manuscripts and pants in need of mending. Quality time between us was spent falling asleep on the couch with our mouths open and our Bibles closed. Days and weeks and months passed with little time made for family devotions, and the new normal in our home became interrupting life to pray rather than interrupting prayer to live.

One day I awoke, that old, familiar horror dawning, but I found no new mercies in the morning, no delight in the work the day would bring. I had come to a shadowy well in my wandering—a dark pit of despair—and like any dumb, self-navigating sheep, I stumbled head-first into the cold waters. I thought to cry out to the Lord, but I was out of practice. His name felt strange on my tongue. How could He even hear me? I had strayed far from His green pasture, and the path of righteousness was a trail grown cold. I was lost and alone and drowning in my despair, and my saturated wool pulled me lower and lower below the water's surface.

But the Good Shepherd chases after the one sheep.

"You have cancer," the doctor told my husband.

I saw that wooden staff coming at me through the water. It hooked me around the neck, dragged me against the slimy rocks, shook me dry, and dropped me on the ground. I stared at the feet of the Shepherd, shocked with shame. No rescue could be more terrifying, more loving.

"What kind of cancer?" I asked. "I don't want him to die."

The Good Shepherd remained silent, but He was with me. I had forgotten that He is always with me, even when I am in a thicket.

The following days, weeks, and months were filled with doctors' visits, diagnostic tests, and latex gloves. We traveled out of state for my husband's surgery (we called it cancer-cation), and we prepared for the subsequent isolation required for his treatment plan. If ever I had forgotten how to call upon the name of the Lord, God gave me the greatest cause to remember.

I am not suggesting that cancer is a cure for what ails me, nor am I intending to color it as something good. I mean only to call the thing what it is: cancer is a horror. It is a horror that gave me cause to call upon God's name, to return to Him in repentance and faith, to remember His goodness and mercy in giving me a husband in the first place. Cancer and its howling jowls chased me back to the safety of the Good Shepherd's pasture where I could rest beside the still waters of God's Word, sit at the table Jesus prepares for me, find comfort in the shadow of His protective staff, and rise each morning fearing no evil. I was unfaithful in my wandering, but God—who is ever faithful—lifted me out of the muck and mire of my own making and set my hooves on His path of righteousness, a path that leads to total trust in His certain love and provision.

Once my husband and I were humbled by our own great need, our eyes grew wise to the Shepherd's abundant, constant care. Family, friends, godchildren, congregation members, fellow pastors, and medical staff—mobilized by the Holy Spirit—rushed to provide for our daily bread. They collected funds, wrote encouraging notes, prayed with and for us, purchased gas and restaurant gift cards for our travels, colored signs to hang in the hospital room, held my husband's hand as he went under in surgery, cut out the vile cancer that threatened his health, kept vigil with me in the waiting room, left voicemails that spoke God's promises into our ears, visited my husband in recovery, counseled and advised us through all of the oncological tests and procedures, and so much more. In being incapable of helping ourselves, we could not miss the countless ways God was helping us through the hands of others.

Strangely, my vocation never changed in all of the fear and fury. Yes, the foster parent certification endeavor promptly ceased, but otherwise, my neighbors—my husband, my family, my church, my children in and out of town—remained there for me to serve. Cancer did not give me fewer people to love, but it did affect the way I chose to take care of them. I began to see them for who they really are—not children in need of a mother, but sheep in need of a Shepherd. I began to strive to be nothing more than a fellow sheep in the flock, a wooly ewe pointing the lambs to trust in Jesus, the Good Shepherd who lays down His life for His sheep[1] and apart from whose blessed care none of us would, or could, exist.

Still, I am tempted to seek satisfaction in the work of my own hands rather than in the faithful care of my Shepherd. Thankfully, Jesus is ever watchful and, in His Word, warns me away from such folly.

One Sabbath, when He was dining with a ruler of the Pharisees, He told a parable[2] of a great banquet, a feast to which the master invited many people. When the time came for the banquet to begin, however, those who were invited began to make excuses.

"I cannot come," one said. "I must see to a field I bought."

"I must take care of my new oxen," said another.

"And I," reasoned another, "already made plans with my new wife."

This is the point in the parable where I insert my own measly excuse: "I am too busy thinking my own thoughts and sorting out my jumbled feelings to feast with you tonight, Master. I fear I won't be much of a companion till I get my head sorted out. Perhaps a raincheck?"

Upon hearing his guests' excuses, the master grows angry and tells his servant to invite the poor, crippled, blind, and lame

---

1   John 10:11
2   Luke 14:15–24

instead. "'Go out to the highways and hedges," he commands, "and compel people to come in, that my home may be filled. For I tell you, none of those men who were invited shall taste my banquet.'"

This parable terrifies me, for I, in my sinful straying, am most definitely one of the idiot invitees too preoccupied to partake of the generous feast. In truth, however, I am also the poor and the crippled and the blind and the lame. I am the castoff sought in the hedges, the sheep brought out of the thicket by the Master's merciful invitation. He sends His servant after me to compel me to feast on the richest food of heaven: Jesus' own body and blood for the forgiveness of my sins.[3] And when I foolishly make excuses? The Good Shepherd comes after me Himself—in this case with cancer—for He keeps His own. Thanks be to God!

I am back in the pasture again, sitting on that cushy, velvety pew, but I am still prone to wander. The difference is that I now know what wandering does. It weathers and felts my wool. It puts me in the path of salivating wolves. It brings me too close to the cliff's edge. It makes me vulnerable to stumbling and drowning. It keeps me from the blessed feast. If nothing else comes from my husband's cancer, I can with confidence confess that God is working this terrible disease for our good by daily reminding us to stay in the pasture where we belong, that we might drink from His still waters, that He might restore our souls.

The Lord is my Shepherd, indeed, and I can hear His voice. I pray that I always will.

> Jesus sinners doth receive;
>   Oh, may all this saying ponder
> Who in sin's delusions live
>   And from God and heaven wander!
> Here is hope for all who grieve:
> Jesus sinners doth receive.

---

3   Matthew 26:26–28

We deserve but grief and shame,
    Yet His words, rich grace revealing,
Pardon, peace, and life proclaim;
    Here our ills have perfect healing.
Firmly in these words believe:
Jesus sinners doth receive.

Sheep that from the fold did stray
    No true shepherd e'er forsaketh;
Weary souls that lost their way
    Christ, the Shepherd, gently taketh
In His arms that they may live:
Jesus sinners doth receive.[4]

---

4   "Jesus Sinners Doth Receive" (stanzas 1–3) by Erdmann Neumeister, tr. *The Lutheran Hymnal*, 1941.

CHAPTER TWO

Fight the Good Fight

by Rebecca Mayes

"I shall not want."
Psalm 23:1

Tracy closed her apartment door behind her, remembering at the last minute that her keys were buried deep in her purse. In order to get them out, she had to rearrange her armful of books and Sunday School supplies. As she did so, a bookmark fluttered to the floor. She glanced down, exasperated at her early morning disorganization, but then had to smile. She had not seen this bookmark for quite some time. Five-year-old Kara had proudly given it to her two years ago—the work of her own hands during craft time in Tracy's class. The coloring and ribbon-tying on the bookmark bore the distinctly youthful marks of Kara's tender efforts, swirls of green and yellow surrounding the typed Bible verse: "Finally, brothers, whatever is true, whatever is honorable, whatever is just, whatever is pure, whatever is lovely, whatever is commendable, if there is any excellence, if there is anything worthy of praise, think about these things."[1]

Tracy was looking forward to thinking about "these things" once she arrived at church that morning. She craved the time to sit, reflect, think, and pray after all the chaos of a hectic work week.

---

1   Philippians 4:8

After pulling into the parking lot, Tracy still had a bit of chaos with which to contend. She headed directly to her Sunday School room to drop off her supplies, but well-meaning church members kept stopping her with greetings and questions about the upcoming potluck she was organizing. Eventually, she found herself in a pew and breathed a sigh of relief to finally be in the Lord's house.

"If we say we have no sin, we deceive ourselves, and the truth is not in us."[2] The familiar words of Scripture spoken by her pastor reverberated throughout the sanctuary.

The congregation was standing, ready to respond in unison. Tracy wondered if she would be challenged this morning to keep focused during the service. As was her habit, she had scanned through the Scripture readings ahead of time to see what the theme of the service would be. Today was Oculi, the third Sunday in Lent—a flood of memories washed over her. It was this same Sunday, years ago, when she had come to some important realizations about who she was, who Christ is, and what all that meant for her life. She smiled at the sudden realization that the Latin word *oculi* means "eyes," a word that would soon be echoed in the words of Psalm 25 from the Introit: "My eyes are ever toward the LORD, for He will pluck my feet out of the net."[3]

Yes, Lord, You certainly opened my eyes, she thought, *and You continue to reveal new mercies to me every week as I come to church to receive Your abundant gifts.*

Tracy joined in on the congregational response, weighing each phrase carefully. "But if we confess our sins, God, who is faithful and just, will forgive our sins and cleanse us from all unrighteousness. . . ."

You are so faithful, Lord Jesus. Faithful and patient. My sin was not something I wanted to confess, even after I realized

---

2   1 John 1:8. The structure of this chapter and occasional excerpts come from the Divine Service on pp. 151–166 in *The Lutheran Service Book* © 2006 Concordia Publishing House. Used with permission. www.cph.org.

3   Psalm 25:15

Your love for me, Your sacrifice for me, Your mercy toward me. I was too ashamed of what I had done, but You chased after me anyway with Your Word. You opened up to me the whole story of redemption—my redemption—captured in the Scriptures.[4] *Thank You for Your Holy Spirit and His work in opening my eyes to Your love shown to me on the cross. Thank You for seeking me, a lost sheep, and laying down Your life to pay for my sins.*

". . . we confess that we are by nature sinful and unclean . . ."

Lord, thank You for putting Bryan and the other members of that Bible study in my life at just the right time! Thank You for giving Bryan the message I needed to hear the most. His knowledge of Your Word and his kindness and honesty were exactly what I'd been missing from the other Christians who kept insisting, "You were not born this way." I knew what I felt and what I'd struggled with for years. No one else would even acknowledge my feelings and admit that they were real. Bryan did.

I'll never forget the confusion—and then relief—when he explained everything so clearly.

"Of course you were born this way. The Bible says, 'I was brought forth in iniquity, and in sin did my mother conceive me.'[5] *We are all born with sin, and we all have sins that are more prominent than others. You've admitted that yours is your attraction to other women. I know it's something you are trying to fight, and it must be difficult. But remember that you're not alone. All Christians are, or rather should be, battling the sins that tempt them. Think about an alcoholic, someone who overeats to deal with depression, or, to be honest, just about every man you've ever met—almost all of us struggle with sexual temptation. Those of us who choose to battle against such temptations have to work at it every day.*

---

4   Romans 5:7–10
5   Psalm 51:5

"One of the verses I think on regularly is from Second Timothy: 'Therefore, if anyone cleanses himself from what is dishonorable, he will be a vessel for honorable use, set apart as holy, useful to the master of the house, ready for every good work.'[6] *I want to be useful to the Master. I want my will and life to line up with God's will and His plans for my life. I pray for that every day, so that I can serve Him with both my body and my soul."*

The final phrase of the congregation's confession broke through Tracy's thoughts. "Forgive us, renew us, and lead us, so that we may delight in Your will and walk in Your ways to the glory of Your holy name. Amen."

As her pastor spoke the forgiving words of the absolution, Tracy made the sign of the cross, almost in slow motion, suddenly aware of the invisible mark she and the others around her wore. "We don't get to choose our own crosses," she once had heard the pastor say. Remembering Bryan's words and the pastor's words, she considered how others around her had their own unique struggles and pain—some obvious, some more hidden.

It's easy to see some of the crosses other people carry. Mike will be in a wheelchair the rest of his life. Now that Bob has died, Patty may be alone for her remaining years. And what about the others? Are there some who were "born with" one of my crosses, the temptation kind?

While scanning the crowd, Tracy's eyes rested on a couple sitting a few pews ahead of her. Her thoughts progressed too quickly to hold back.

I wonder if Janine was born with her mouth open, ready to give her opinion to anyone within earshot. And I bet Fred was too stubborn to leave the womb by his due date.

Tracy shut her eyes to block out the visual source of her unhelpful speculations. *Forgive us, renew us, and lead us,* she repeated in earnest.

---

6   2 Timothy 2:21

"Let us pray," the pastor interrupted her confession. "O God, whose glory it is always to have mercy, be gracious to all who have gone astray from Your ways and bring them again with penitent hearts and steadfast faith to embrace and hold fast the unchangeable truth of Your Word; through Jesus Christ, Your Son, our Lord, who lives and reigns with You and the Holy Spirit, one God, now and forever. Amen."

The unchangeable truth of Your Word. That's the phrase that got me the first time I was here. Bryan invited me numerous times to church, and it just happened to be this Oculi Sunday that I agreed to come. That had to be the Holy Spirit's work. I was amazed how everything in the service all tied together, like it was tailored for my situation. The prayer, the readings, the hymns. It was a little frightening, to tell the truth, and certainly too much to take in all at once, but over the years I see more and more how Your Word in the liturgy speaks to troubled souls.

I wasn't guided by Your truth then. My feelings were my compass. I knew You were out there, Lord. At least, I had some concept of You. I knew there was right and wrong. "Right," however, was what felt right, and being with another woman did feel right. It made me happy, and I felt sure that You would want me to be happy.

I wanted affection, affirmation, acceptance. I wanted love. I thought I knew what love was, but I didn't—not Your love, Lord. Not Your bloody, sacrificial love that endured torture to save even Your enemies. My feelings were inconsistent, as were those of my partners, and the hurt was intense. I longed for something that didn't change, for a love that didn't ebb and flow. I learned that Your love is forever.

The possibility that You loved me—truly loved me—was what led me to the Bible study at school. The genuine Christian kindness I found there from Bryan and the others was what prepared me to hear Your whole truth—who I was as a sinner and who I was as a precious child of the Heavenly Father.

Tracy listened intently to the Old Testament lesson about Moses, the plagues of gnats and flies, and Pharaoh's hardened heart in refusing to listen to those who told him, "This is the finger of God."[7]

Then the pastor began to read from Ephesians: "Therefore be imitators of God, as beloved children. And walk in love, as Christ loved us and gave Himself up for us . . ." It was the same convicting Epistle reading Tracy had heard all those years ago. "But sexual immorality and all impurity or covetousness must not even be named among you, as is proper among saints. Let there be no filthiness nor foolish talk nor crude joking, which are out of place, but instead let there be thanksgiving."[8]

> *It took me months before I accepted Bryan's invitation to church and heard the Law of God read so clearly during the Epistle lesson. By that time, I knew I wanted You in my life, Lord, and I knew I trusted You. You planted the seeds, slowly and carefully, to prepare me for just the right moment to hear the gravity of my sin and the bountifulness of Your mercy.*
>
> *I had heard this kind of moral instruction from well-meaning Christian friends before, but for some reason it only turned me away. It was all true—I know that now—but I wasn't in the right mindset to receive it. I already felt unloved and judged. You, Lord, knew I needed Your love before I could honestly look at my sin.*

In the Gospel reading, Tracy heard Jesus cast out a mute demon, speak more of the finger of God, and paint the image of the strong man guarding his own palace.[9] Then, as the congregation joined in singing a hymn, Tracy noticed something

---

7   Exodus 8:16–24
8   Ephesians 5:1–4
9   Luke 11:14–28

new in the sacred poetry—a theme within the service she had never caught before.

> Lord, be our light when worldly darkness veils us;
> Lord, be our shield when earthly armor fails us;
> And in the day when hell itself assails us,
>   Grant us Your peace, Lord.
>
> Peace in our hearts, where sinful thoughts are raging,
> Peace in Your Church, our troubled souls assuaging,
> Peace when the world its endless war is waging,
>   Peace in Your heaven.[10]

As Tracy's mind pondered the hymn's stark contrast between tranquility and chaos, the pastor approached the pulpit to preach the sermon. He used no gentle introduction or lead-in story. He had a message to share and chose to get right to the point.

"Satan is the strong man from whom you cannot free yourself. Armed with the mighty weapons of lies and temptations, he guards his palace with the demands and accusations of the Law, with pride, contempt, sin, and death. You can neither pierce his armor nor stand against his weapons. You are surrounded, afflicted, assaulted, and tempted by more demonic flies and gnats than you could possibly number."[11]

Yes, I know, I know!

"Do not harden your heart like Pharaoh of old or like Jesus' opponents. If you claim to be a Christian but still give in to, indulge, and delight in filthiness and crude and foolish talk, sexual immorality and impurity, covetousness and idolatry; if you return to lust, greed, and anger; if you despise your brother in Christ, you are a partner with darkness who will die. So you must discipline and mortify your flesh. Surrender all, even the world, honor, and possessions. Return to the Lord in repentance

---

10 "Lord of Our Life" (stanzas 3–4) by Matthäus Apelles von Löwenstern, tr. Philip Pusey.

11 The sermon portions are from Lent 3—Oculi 2018 by Rev. Ron Stephens. www.cyberstones.org (accessed June 7, 2018).

and contrition. Confess your sins and call upon the name of the Lord Jesus."

> *There are always so many sins to confess, yet this sin against the flesh is more dangerous than others.[12] I have to acknowledge that, still.*
>
> *Thank you for never leaving me alone, Lord, without ways to divert my mind. I've noticed Your help time and again. First it was that core group from the campus Bible study. Their strong convictions were the shield I needed at the time. I felt so safe in their presence. They helped me find new sources of joy, like studying the Word, serving others, and nurturing the family ties and relationships I had neglected. I was so busy back then, but I needed that. This congregation is also a blessed gift from You. Thank You for these loving people who bear with me in love, even with all of their flaws and imperfections. You know exactly what I need, and You provide for me every step of the way.*
>
> *You've helped me develop a discipline of regularly being in the Word that gets me through each day now. I know if I neglect reading the Bible, even for a short while, my flesh gets weaker and the battle against temptation gets harder. What is that verse that goes, "For the Word of God is . . . sharper than any two-edged sword"?[13] I think that's it.*

Tracy's mind suddenly recalled the Sunday School coloring page from several months ago that featured the armor of God. The image was as clear as if she were holding it in front of her: the belt of truth, the breastplate of righteousness, the shield of faith, the helmet of salvation, and the sword of the Spirit.[14]

> *Thank You for the weapons You've given me—given all of us! I wonder, though, if anyone else gets as tired as I do on the battlefield?*

---

12   1 Corinthians 6:18–20
13   Hebrews 4:12
14   Ephesians 6:14–17

I see that You are helping others here, too, in this very congregation. I see them disciplining and mortifying their flesh by not always giving into their emotions and natural tendencies. You come to their aid like You come to mine by reminding us that what we feel and what comes naturally to us can, in fact, be harmful to ourselves and those around us. When Janine held her tongue at the voters' meeting during that dispute last month, I knew that she was fighting to listen before she spoke. In the end, she was victorious, because her silence allowed the full facts to be presented and misunderstandings were cleared up. You got her through that and blessed everyone in the process.

Later that evening, I also heard Fred apologize to the pastor for his part in perpetuating a particular conflict in the congregation. That must have been so hard for him to do, but with Your help, he did it. I see the Holy Spirit at work in the lives of Your people. Thank You, Lord.

Oh, no! How much of the sermon have I missed?

"Behold: the Stronger Man, Jesus Christ, has come," the pastor continued. "God comes armored in human flesh and wielding no weapon but the Spirit—the Finger of God. Though His armor was pierced through and He was dead, though it seemed the devil had won, the pierced heel of Jesus came raining down from the cross. The devil's head was crushed, his jaw broken, and his lying tongue severed. Satan's armor was worthless and his weapons impotent, destroyed from the inside out by the wood of Jesus' cross."

The pastor's detailed imagery captured Tracy's vivid imagination, and she could not help but picture herself standing in the middle of this spiritual battlefield, the carnage lying all around her. Her mind's eye lingered on the grotesque, severed tongue of the father of lies.

"By the Spirit, Jesus touches your eyes, opening them to see by faith, and loosens your tongue that you may open your lips to praise Him, confess His name, and confess your sins. Like the mute man before you, your tongue is now loosed and you give thanks and praise to Him who saved you. You now walk as a child of the Light, for Jesus' own perfect righteousness covers you. You are the imitator of God, for Christ dwells in you in His body and blood. The devil dwells in you no more. You belong to the Stronger Man and are a new creation in Him."

> *I am understanding more and more how You can take what Satan meant for evil and use it for good. Janine's mouth now often pours forth words filled with encouragement and praise, especially for the young families here who need this so much. Fred's unbending character serves his unyielding commitment to the Scriptures and our Church's doctrine. What a positive influence his fortitude has been to the other men in the congregation. Yes, both of these saints and their struggles have been used for good.*
>
> *Has my cross been used for good? Can something good come from my fight against sexual temptation? I guess You've given me the ability to see through people's self-made walls and masks more easily than most, whether inside or outside the Church. I can certainly relate to their battles with sin and, therefore, love and forgive them more readily, knowing how much I've been forgiven. I can see the child of God in each of them. These are good things, aren't they?*

"Yes, you must struggle against sin and the lusts of your flesh. But your struggle is not hopeless. You are in Jesus Christ. And though Satan still tempts you, seeking to deceive and mislead you, Jesus beats him down under your feet. He cannot and will not have you. The Stronger Man has overcome. The peace of God, which passes all understanding, keep your hearts and minds in Christ Jesus. Amen."

There it was, the reminder of the theme Tracy had noticed earlier: peace. It came up again and again throughout the rest of the service, as though the liturgy following the sermon was created to make this final point to the sinner.

"The peace of the Lord be with you always," the pastor said before communion began.

The congregation then sang in thankful response to the Holy Supper, "Lord, now You let Your servant go in peace."

"The Lord look upon you with favor," the pastor spoke a final blessing over his flock, "and give you peace."

Peace! How have I not noticed this before?

Yes, peace is the desired outcome of every battle. It's the outcome I long for in my own battle against sexual temptation. You, Lord, promise me eternal peace of heart, soul, and mind in the end, but even now You provide moments of earthly peace over and over again, in many and various ways. You give me a foretaste of the eternal peace that follows this fight—a fight St. Paul tells me is good,[15] despite how hard it is.

Oh, come, Lord, come quickly, so we may all lay down our weapons and rest.

> Fight the good fight with all your might;
> Christ is your strength, and Christ your right.
>   Lay hold on life, and it shall be
>   Your joy and crown eternally.
>
> Cast care aside, lean on your guide;
> His boundless mercy will provide.
>   Trust, and enduring faith shall prove
>   Christ is your life and Christ your love.[16]

---

15   2 Timothy 4:7
16   "Fight the Good Fight" (stanzas 1, 3) by John S. B. Monsell.

CHAPTER THREE

What Shall I Render to the Lord?
by Kantor Christina Roberts

"He makes me lie down in green pastures."
Psalm 23:2

kantor: n. [ˈkan.tər, ˈkahn.tər] a person with musical and theological training responsible for facilitating the congregation's song. Tasks may include, but are not limited to: playing organ, directing choirs, organizing instrumentalists, selecting hymnody, composing new music, researching copyright law, filing scores, building bulletins, prodding unwilling tenors, reining in overzealous sopranos, keeping a store of screwdrivers at hand for last minute handbell repair, fastening robes on wiggling lads, signaling an usher to ring the bell so services begin on time, making judicious use of a rearview mirror to provide neither too many nor too few distribution hymns, and teaching everything from quarter notes to Bach's cantatas.

The choir children at my church seem to take pleasure in leading (read: misleading) me into meandering conversations. They typically begin with an innocent enough question; for instance, "What is your favorite Sunday of the church year, Kantor?" I unwittingly walk right into their snare, failing to see that what inevitably follows is an inquiry into my *least* favorite Sunday. Like a mother ranking her own children, I, in poor taste, drop Palm Sunday in the bottom tier.

To deflect all immediate scandals and schisms, I launch into a stand-up routine detailing our congregation's Palm Sunday tradition of processing outside around our bell-less bell tower. The journey is replete with wind-whipped stoles and skirts, young choristers sword fighting with palm fronds, and accidental tempo changes in "All Glory, Laud, and Honor."[1] The story usually brings about laughter in the listener, but in reality, my Palm Sunday spoof is a dark comedy that serves to reinforce my lackluster opinion of the day.

Actually, once we get beyond the awkward procession at the beginning of the service, Palm Sunday settles into an extended reading of St. Matthew's Passion, and the simplicity of the rest of the service captures my heart by imprinting on it the image of Jesus crucified for me.[2] This sets the stage for the next six days of Holy Week, which I adore. Until Easter, that is.

Here is where I admit that I am not being entirely forthright with the choir children—or myself—when I list Palm Sunday as the least-favored child. Easter is, in fact, the Sunday I struggle with the most.

Easter arrives with heightened expectations and elevated pitch. The gold paraments blind. The lily scent suffocates. The bells ring, the brass fanfare, the choirs descant. I, not figuratively but literally, pull out all the stops until the sounds of organ and voices deafen. At this point, my mouth purses at the abundance of stimuli.

"I'm just exhausted."

I offer up this line, nearly as well-rehearsed as my postlude, over Easter breakfast eggs to squelch questions about my lack of singing and somber demeanor. The heart of the problem, though, is not just that my body needs more sleep; it is that my body,

---

1   "All Glory, Laud, and Honor" by Theodulf of Orléans, tr. John Mason Neale.
2   "On My Heart Imprint Your Image" by Thomas Hansen Kingo, tr. Peer O. Strömme.

mind, and soul are wearied—wearied and heavy laden[3] with my own sins, the faults and troubles of those around me, and worries for the future.

I am uncomfortable with rejoicing. Hope makes me nervous. Happiness feels false. Freedom stuns me into indecision. Give me back my Lent. The days of quiet, dark, rigid fasting seem a safe retreat from the unpredictable and unfettered exuberance around me.

O Lord, open my lips,[4] for I have slammed them shut.

By now, any healthy, well-adjusted human being is asking, "Who doesn't like Easter? What's wrong with this woman?" Just as I hesitate to admit that the services celebrating the resurrection of our Lord overwhelm me, I am also reluctant to let others know that I struggle with depression. No official diagnosis of depression or mental illness is checked on my medical chart (save a postpartum visit), but feelings of doubt, anxiety, isolation, despair, and futility are well-known to me.

Maybe you know them too. They were never a part of God's original plan for creation. Before that infamous bite of fruit,[5] Eve didn't struggle with whether or not to refill the Zoloft prescription. Adam didn't stay home from tending the animals because he just couldn't get out of bed. In the beginning, they walked nude and free in the garden—no shame, no anxiety, no despair, none of it.

Sin and Satan entered our world and immediately the saints of old struggled against joy. The tear-stained throw pillows of the psalmist[6] serve as evidence that we are not alone in our nightly plight of bawling. The Israelites asked for their good, old graves back in Egypt rather than continuing in the promises of God.[7] Forget frogs and grasshoppers—they, like us, were plagued with doubt, anxiety, isolation, despair, and feelings of futility.

---

3   Matthew 11:28
4   Psalm 51:15
5   Genesis 3:1–7
6   Psalm 6:6
7   Exodus 14:11

Whether or not we have a depression diagnosis, we all toil under the weight of failings, real or perceived. We fight against God's call to serve others. We are lonely and afflicted and still manage to blow the troubles of our hearts wildly out of proportion.[8]

Despite having all of this in common with my Old Testament brothers and sisters, I cannot fully comprehend their suffering. I cannot fully comprehend yours either. And it is not your fault that mine is a mystery to you.

A kantor's work is to sing and make music to the Lord. To the world, maybe even to the once-in-a-while worshiper, this job description begs to be typed in cartoonish fonts adorned with colorful eighth notes on a swishy staff. Everyone can hear the kazoo choir making a joyful noise as the soundtrack to my life. Thanks be to God, this is not my reality. In truth, my job provides very little in the way of saccharin happiness. That suits me, though, as do the blessings that abound.

What often eludes public perception is what blessings look like in the life of a church musician. For those who are confused into thinking that a posture of joy is modeled by an upturned beaming face and outstretched arms spinning upon a mountain precipice at sunrise, the actual physical responses to our Lord's gifts may surprise. His blessings bring me joy, but the joy is often hard to see.

In me, joy sharply inhales a breath as the Sunday schoolers unexpectedly break into a descant at the words, "Open-eyed my grave is staring: Even there I'll sleep secure."[9] Joy lumps in my throat as the congregation sings "Lamb of God, Pure and Holy"[10] *a cappella* and in balanced four-part harmony. Joy keeps a stoic face as monotone gentlemen belt out their songs to the Lord. Joy foolishly gives a conducting cue to a blind soloist singing the day's Introit: "My eyes are ever toward the LORD."[11] Joy blurs my

---

8   Psalm 25:16–17

9   "God's Own Child, I Gladly Say It" (stanza 5) by Erdmann Neumeister, tr. Robert E. Voelker. Used with permission.

10   "Lamb of God, Pure and Holy" by Nicolaus Decius, tr. *The Lutheran Hymnal,* 1941.

11   Psalm 25:15

vision as muscle memory takes over playing organ at a beloved sister's funeral. Joy holds a dear friend's hand in the middle of a bustling cookie exchange while she gives me the hymn list for her funeral "just in case" she doesn't make it through the next day's cancer surgery.

Joy isn't written in **Comic Sans**, but it is written all over my job description.

I'm convinced that the Lord made me a kantor with its Gospel-saturated duties so that I would always, especially in the most difficult portions of life, be immersed in His Word. The most demanding weeks of my job are also the ones in which nearly every working moment is focused on the Holy Scriptures. Christ's promises of forgiveness, life, and salvation are in the subtext of every line on my to-do list.

The Lord has also provided an arsenal of worldly weapons that help with depression: talk therapy, medication, exercise, mindfulness techniques, scheduling strategies, nutritional plans, sunlight simulators, Pandora playlists, happiness podcasts, essential oils, vitamin regimens, and the like. I pray that He gives me wisdom to choose and use these earthly gifts[12] so that I may serve others with love and compassion. I pray that He gives you wisdom to use them too.

But what I really want for you is what my job as a kantor daily provides for me: an abundance of Jesus, because it is the forgiveness, life, and salvation earned by His death and resurrection that is

---

12   We Lutherans like to refer to any earthly benefit as First Article gifts, referring to the First Article of the Apostles' Creed: "I believe in God, the Father Almighty, maker of heaven and earth." Dr. Martin Luther detailed these gifts in the explanation of this article in his catechism: "*What does this mean?* I believe that God has made me and all creatures; that He has given me my body and soul, eyes, ears, and all my members, my reason and all my senses, and still takes care of them. He also gives me clothing and shoes, food and drink, house and home, wife and children, land, animals, and all I have. He richly and daily provides me with all that I need to support this body and life. He defends me against all danger and guards and protects me from all evil. All this He does only out of fatherly, divine goodness and mercy, without any merit or worthiness in me. For all this it is my duty to thank and praise, serve and obey Him. This is most certainly true." From *Luther's Small Catechism with Explanation* © 1986, 1991 Concordia Publishing House. Used with permission. www.cph.org.

our cure.[13] Rev. Todd Peperkorn reassures us of this: "The Gospel will do its work even if the person receiving it doesn't know it or doesn't feel it or doesn't show it."[14]

This promise of the Gospel's sure and certain work is of immense comfort to a church musician who at times blankly stares her way through the words, "In Thee is gladness amid all sadness."[15] My failure to know, feel, and show His mercy acting upon me is far deeper than I will ever realize, but in retrospect, I do see some of those lush pastures in which our Shepherd has placed me. At first, my mental afflictions cause me to identify these spots as dry, scraggly, briar-filled patches. But the Lord, through His Word and song, causes me to lie down and see seemingly ugly patches as they really are: His gifts of mercy, peace, and comfort to a foolish lamb struggling against the One who loves her and saves her from herself.

I may scowl my way through the interrupting alleluias of "Jesus Christ Is Risen Today,"[16] yet by the time we have gotten to the third stanza, He has already made the triumphant day ours, suffered to redeem our loss, and endured the cross and grave all to procure our salvation. Then, just to top it all off in the fourth stanza, He smacks a big baptismal reminder on our foreheads with the name of the Triune God: Father, Son, and Holy Ghost.

13   Here, we look to Dr. Luther's words in the explanation of the Second Article of the Apostles' Creed: *"What does this mean?* I believe that Jesus Christ, true God, begotten of the Father from eternity, and also true man, born of the Virgin Mary, is my Lord, who has redeemed me, a lost and condemned person, purchased and won me from all sins, from death, and from the power of the devil; not with gold or silver, but with His holy, precious blood and with His innocent suffering and death, that I may be His own and live under Him in His kingdom and serve Him in everlasting righteousness, innocence, and blessedness, just as He is risen from the dead, lives and reigns to all eternity. This is most certainly true." From *Luther's Small Catechism with Explanation* © 1986, 1991 Concordia Publishing House. Used with permission. www.cph.org.

14   Todd Peperkorn, "Making the Case for a Lutheran View of Depression." Presentation, Issues, Etc., Making the Case Conference, Collinsville, Illinois, June 10, 2017.

15   "In Thee Is Gladness" by Johann Lindemann, tr. Catherine Winkworth.

16   "Jesus Christ Is Risen Today" (stanzas 1–3) Latin text, tr. *Lyra Davidica*; (stanza 4) by Charles Wesley.

Do I know it, feel it, or show it? Maybe. Maybe not. Is salvation mine? Absolutely. Alleluia times sixteen.

The truth remains that when it is Easter, I want Lent. Yet oddly enough, during Lent, I crave Easter. In the heat of the summer as the green season of the church year drags, I long for the excitement of Christ's advent and incarnation. Then, when the busy days of Christmas celebrations are in full swing, I wish we could slow down and reflect on our Lord's teachings with fewer distractions. I don't know what I need or when I need it, but the Lord does. His life shapes my calendar.[17] His life gives my life structure. His life is my life.

Do I know it, feel it, or show it? Sometimes. Sometimes not. Has He formed my days[18] anyway? Absolutely. So, I continue singing with the psalmist, "How precious to me are Your thoughts, O God!"[19]

Prone to let my inner dialogue belittle my true worth in Christ, I can lose countless hours of life reliving past mistakes in my mind. The voice in my head is loud and relentless. If left to my own devices, I drown it out with even nastier self-talk. Gladly, one of the hazards of any job in music is the endless supply of earworms, those tunes that stick in your head and replay *ad nauseam*. Our hymns and liturgies circulate through my mind seven days a week, washing away the accusatory, one-sided conversation of doubt and anxiety. Christ's new song drowns out the harsh lies and reminds me of the clean conscience I possess through His Son's blood. Jesus speaks to us through His Word, and in the Church, that blessed Word is often attached to the gift of music. That music plants its roots in our memories, and we can hear Him speak—sing—to us all day long.

Do I know, feel, and show that I am listening? Yes. No.

---

17   As a liturgical church body, we Lutherans schedule our worship and lives around the life of Christ. The calendar of the church year is structured with seasons to walk through Jesus' anticipated coming, birth, life, suffering, death, resurrection, ascension, the sending of the Holy Spirit, and the life of the Church.

18   Psalm 139:16

19   Psalm 139:17

Does the Lord mute His earworms? Never.

"Lord, to whom shall we go? You have the words of eternal life."[20] Amen.

Just the slightest cold will rob my asthmatic lungs of air and my vocal folds of vibration. Yet, even though my voice is silenced, the Lord lives and grants me daily breath[21] through the intonations of others. In our faculty devotions, I silently plead, "In the morning, O LORD, You hear my voice,"[22] and He does, as the sounds of our pastors and teachers reach His ear. Later in the day, the school children sing their confession, "We all believe in one true God, who created earth and heaven . . ."[23] And although I am unable to navigate the melismatic creed, the students include me in the corporate pronoun "we." At the close of an evening rehearsal, after my choir has suffered through squawks and hand signals to prepare the music for church, they graciously lend me their voices for one last close-of-day prayer, "Into Your hands, O LORD, I commend my spirit."[24]

My choir is not the first to sing those words for me. Despite His parched lips and crushed lungs, our Savior cried out that prayer from the cross. He wasn't battling a little cold. He was in "a strange and dreadful strife," with life and death contending.[25] Contending for me. Battling for you. In the midst of the combat, Jesus went to His hymnal, the Book of Psalms, to receive the comfort of the promises that He, the Triune God, made.

I love to ponder the possibility that Jesus *sang* the loud cries of Psalms 22 and 31 from the cross, just as He most likely had sung them over His thirty-three years. That may be nothing more than pious conjecture, but it is not guesswork to say that God has given us those words to sing in both life and death. Nor is it beyond what we know from Scripture to say that the Lord indeed sings over us:

---

20   John 6:68
21   "I Know that My Redeemer Lives" (stanza 7) by Samuel Medley.
22   Psalm 5:3
23   "We All Believe in One True God" (stanza 1) by Martin Luther, tr. *The Lutheran Hymnal.*
24   Psalm 31:5
25   "Christ Jesus Lay in Death's Strong Bands" (stanza 4) by Martin Luther, tr. Richard Massie.

"Fear not, O Zion;
    let not your hands grow weak.
The LORD your God is in your midst,
    a mighty one who will save;
He will rejoice over you with gladness;
    He will quiet you by His love;
He will exult over you with loud singing."[26]

Do I know my Lord is singing? Do I feel His glad rejoicing? Do I show strength in my hands? I do, because His Word tells me it is so, even though I sometimes want to plug my ears, look away from His shining countenance, and let my fingers quake. The Lord's promises are true. He sings over me. He sings over you too.

All these gracious benefits are ours, and what do we sinners give to the Lord? Instead of letting us anxiously flounder in our inability to decide, Psalm 116 tells us exactly what the Lord desires:

What shall I render to the LORD
    for all His benefits to me?
I will lift up the cup of salvation
    and call on the name of the LORD . . .
I will offer to You the sacrifice of thanksgiving
    and call on the name of the LORD.
I will pay my vows to the LORD
    in the presence of all His people,
in the courts of the house of the LORD,
    in your midst, O Jerusalem. Praise the LORD![27]

The Lord wants us to lift up the cup of salvation. Gladly, we do not even have to muster the strength to do that lifting. Christ drank from the cup of God's wrath for us, so that we can drink from the chalice of blessing the pastor holds before our lips. Drink deeply of that which was poured out for the forgiveness of your sins.[28] We are invited to the Lord's Table every time it is spread. Let us not miss out on an opportunity to join in the Feast. Our eternal life has already begun. Be at the celebration.

---

26   Zephaniah 3:16–17
27   Psalm 116:12–13, 17–19
28   Matthew 26:28

The Lord also longs to hear you call on His name. Pray for yourself and for others. When you experience paralysis of heart and tongue like me, return to the words He has given you to pray: Lord, have mercy. Christ, have mercy. Lord, have mercy.[29] Our Father, who art in heaven.[30]

Open the Psalms, and do not let the sheer number of them overwhelm you. Start in the depths of Psalm 130. Beg the Lord to lift up your soul with Psalm 25. Visit Psalm 32 and remember, O blessed one, your sins are covered. In the middle of the night when you, like the author of Psalm 88, are awakened, do not toss and turn in dread. Give your foreboding over to Christ who will present your prayers to the Father. He promises always to hear you, and He will.

The Lord also wishes for us to offer the sacrifice of thanksgiving. Eyes shaded by a dark worldview often find it difficult to see much for which to be thankful. Look to Jesus on the cross who, under the shadow of that Good Friday, overcame all the bleakness of our lives. Knowing God's love through the gift of His Son helps to shape gratitude for even the simplest of this world's gifts: every sip of coffee, autumnal tree, well-crafted movie score, or shared glance with a beloved. Above all, we offer thanksgiving by taking from the Lord what He wants to give. Take His absolution[31] to heart. Take His name, given at Baptism,[32] into every moment of the day. Take, eat and drink His body and blood for the forgiveness of your sins.[33]

Finally, the Lord asks for us to pay our vows to Him in the presence of His people. What vow can we sinners possibly make and endeavor to keep? In repentance and faith, we look instead to the vow the Lord has made to us. In Baptism, He vowed to be our Savior,[34] to wash us clean of all our sin,[35] to give us eternal life with Him.[36] Suddenly, our vow makes sense. We vow to receive

---

29   Mark 10:47
30   Matthew 6:9–13
31   John 20:19–23
32   Matthew 28:19
33   Matthew 26:26; 1 Corinthians 11:24
34   Isaiah 43:3
35   Psalm 51:2
36   John 3:16

these marvelous gifts in faith, and we believe that even this is done by the grace of God.[37]

Finally, let a sullen kantor who often wants nothing more than to be alone remind you that Jesus has asked us to receive these gifts in the presence of His people. Join the Body of Christ. Join the choir. Join with me in working to increase your personal collection of divine earworms, and sing—in full voice, for we have full forgiveness—for the sake of others who need the cure of Christ.

There may be many days when the idea of facing a crowd of people decked out in their Sunday finest seems insurmountable. Go to church anyway. Hide behind the hymnal with me, tuck your face into the Bible, and listen as your brothers and sisters in Christ sing to you of Jesus' death and resurrection. He has not designed us to bear our burdens alone.

> For you have promised, Lord, to heed
> Your children's cries in time of need
>   Through Him whose name alone is great,
>   Our Savior and our advocate.
>
> And so we come, O God, today
> And all our woes before You lay;
>   For sorely tried, cast down, we stand,
>   Perplexed by fears on ev'ry hand.
>
> O from our sins, Lord, turn Your face;
> Absolve us through Your boundless grace.
>   Be with us in our anguish still;
>   Free us at last from ev'ry ill.
>
> So we with all our hearts each day
> To You our glad thanksgiving pay,
>   Then walk obedient to Your Word,
>   And now and ever praise You, Lord.[38]

---

37 Ephesians 2:8
38 "When in the Hour of Deepest Need" (stanzas 3–6) by Paul Eber, tr. Catherine Winkworth.

CHAPTER FOUR

Motherhood and Mental Illness

by Cheryl Swope

"He leads me beside still waters."
Psalm 23:2

We Said, "No, Thank You."

When we applied to become adoptive parents, my husband and I checked one box to indicate the one condition we could not handle: mental illness. The adoption workers wanted to achieve the best possible placement, so they asked us to be honest. We were. We did not know much about parenting, but we knew we could not handle mental illness.

We understood that mental illness could be irrational, unpredictable, and frightening. We concluded that this would require parents who were inherently level-headed, predictable, self-sacrificing, and loving. With ample self-knowledge, we resolutely checked "no" to mental illness.

No one read our form.

Rachel, the case worker, told us months later that if anyone *had* read our form, our children never would have been placed with us. Miraculously slipping through the cracks and into our arms, fair-headed, thirteen-month-old twin babies entered our lives. With the children would come many unknowns.

Be still, my soul; the Lord is on your side;
 Bear patiently the cross of grief or pain;
Leave to your God to order and provide;
 In ev'ry change He faithful will remain.
Be still, my soul; your best, your heav'nly Friend
Through thorny ways leads to a joyful end.[1]

Early Childhood

The social worker explained that the twins' biological mother had paranoid schizophrenia. Despite a vague sense of foreboding, we gratefully embraced the little ones in our arms. I had prayed for these children long before I knew them, and I loved them dearly. When I gazed into the clear, blue eyes of my beautiful children, I felt only warmth and love. The words spoken earlier to me, "The children have a higher risk of developing schizophrenia," seemed impossibly far away.

An early sign of trouble came when little Michael banged his toddler forehead fervently on our hardwood floors. His foster parents noted only that the baby "had a temper," but when I arranged playdates for Michael to help compensate for his social difficulties, he either threw toys at the other child or simply ignored the bewildered playmate. In his best moments, however, Michael was my dream child. He could be engaging, thoughtful, and full of wonder. He soaked up learning and was a joy to teach. I marveled at the disparity. His speech was often lax and unintelligible. Moody undercurrents sometimes moved in angry waves, as they did one afternoon during a family photo under my grandmother's large shade tree. Four-year-old Michael was inconsolable and went to bed. My keenly perceptive grandma pulled me aside. "I think you need to take him to a psychiatrist." She was right. Over the next few years my son's first diagnoses would be autism and mood disorder.

Michelle, his twin sister, maintained a bright and cheery countenance but alarmed us in other ways. She scurried to high

---

1 "Be Still My Soul" (stanza 1) by Catharina Amalia Dorothea von Schlegel, tr. Jane L. Borthwick.

walls if left unattended and spoke with marked oddity in both her words and her intonation. Remarkably loud, Michelle enunciated clearly, but at times her language made little sense. With crystal blue eyes that melted my heart but sometimes seemed to look through me, as is common in autism, Michelle's mind and body tumbled with her own waves and winds. Often Michelle had dangerous cravings for non-food items like detergent, liquid soap, and glass cleaner. My daughter's first diagnoses were autism, semantic-pragmatic language disorder, pica, and ADHD.

Perhaps it was my master's degree in special education, or perhaps it was my growing love for these children, but I found that I could achieve more with both of them than other adults did. And so, along with taking the children to physical, occupational, speech, and language therapies, I taught them at home. From infancy, both of them were captivated by songs and stories. They loved books, and we loved reading to them. We settled into a gentle routine. Our favorite family times became going to church, reading books throughout the day, and praying together before bedtime. We found that both children responded well to a calm, predictable structure with plenty of nurturing.

Within those brief few years of the children's early childhood, we had bonded to them, and they to us. We knew other adoptive situations in which this was not the case, so we were thankful for this.

> Be still, my soul; your God will undertake
>   To guide the future as He has the past.
> Your hope, your confidence let nothing shake;
>   All now mysterious shall be bright at last.
> Be still, my soul; the waves and winds still know
> His voice who ruled them while He dwelt below.[2]

SCHOOL AGE

My husband and I believed that a strong classical Christian education would become their greatest ally, but in addition

---

2   "Be Still My Soul" (stanza 2) by Catharina Amalia Dorothea von Schlegel, tr. Jane L. Borthwick.

to the challenges described above, both children displayed specific learning disabilities. Michael could not process spoken information rapidly, his speech continued to be garbled at times, and he could not sustain attention or concentration. Michelle's handwriting at age six appeared like a child's three years younger, she had profound difficulties in arithmetic, and her oral language remained aberrant.

Throughout their education both children studied Latin, and Michael developed a love of history while Michelle became enchanted by poetic language, especially Shakespeare. Poems were brimming in her mind and spilling onto paper. In many ways the children exceeded expectations placed upon them by birth, circumstances, and experts. This is, in fact, what prompted me to write *Simply Classical: A Beautiful Education for Any Child* and to create the Simply Classical Curriculum, so that others who longed to give their children with special needs a beautiful education could do so.[3]

As the children began to achieve, learn, and grow in the quiet of our home, I dared to hope that we might avert schizophrenia altogether. Michael's love of history and literature evidenced a maturing mind elevated by heroes and heroic themes. Under the guidance of an exceptional leader, he worked in our French colonial town's history museum and learned to appreciate first-hand the doctrine of vocation, God's calling in all of work. We rejoiced with Michael and Michelle in their courage amidst the trials. We persisted.

I began earnestly to study the subject of schizophrenia, as if my knowledge could further counter the genetic predisposition. Yet one evening when I read about the strong heritable nature of mental illness I realized, perhaps for the first time, that their unknown biological father, and possibly his family, might have

---

3   Cheryl Swope, *Simply Classical: A Beautiful Education for Any Child* (Louisville: Memoria Press, 2013). This book details the story of how tried-and-true teaching helped both Michael and Michelle overcome many of the challenges they faced with learning. Although neither child seemed like a good candidate for studying Latin, literature, or logic, both benefited tremendously in ways we see even today.

had mental illness too. I was reminded that the dreaded malady could appear at any time.

There were continued signs of something more than mere autism or learning disabilities. Social difficulties became more prominent as the children grew older. Michael's mood swings and Michelle's mental disorganization strained childhood friendships beyond other children's compassion and understanding. Both Michael and Michelle exhibited paranoia, such as suspecting that the carefree children in our homeschool 4-H group were secretly plotting against them. During these years we often cringed for them, as we learned the ache of parents who watch their children feel social isolation. At the same time we found less and less in common with our own peers, parents whose children seemed to breeze effortlessly through childhood. We determined to make the most of the lonely situation by enriching the four lives in our home. We studied together, we camped, we hiked, we played games, we read long books, we attended church, and we prayed.

> Be still, my soul; though dearest friends depart
>   And all is darkened in this vale of tears;
> Then you will better know His love, His heart,
>   Who comes to soothe your sorrows and your fears.
> Be still, my soul; your Jesus can repay
> From His own fullness all He takes away.[4]

IMPOSSIBLE TO IGNORE

Michael's troubling mood disorder turned to blatant aggression, and he began hearing a voice commentating on his daily actions. One morning after Michael asked me, "May I have some cereal?", he smiled in an odd way because he then heard a seemingly external, robotic voice saying, "'*May I have some cereal?' the boy asked.*" He told me that he began to see large signs of words at night displaying random thoughts. When radio announcers laughed on air, he became agitated because he thought they were laughing at

---

4   "Be Still My Soul" (stanza 3) by Catharina Amalia Dorothea von Schlegel, tr. Jane L. Borthwick.

him. He regressed in his studies and could not manage daily tasks. His spatial perception was askew to where he would mistake a flat surface as slanting, and he grew concerned because he could not tell where to place his feet. Michael became gravely depressed and told me he wanted to go straight to heaven.

After frustrating false starts with counselors who missed the gravity of the situation, we received assistance from a local psychiatrist. Though inexperienced with schizophrenia and unwilling to make such a diagnosis, she recognized his autism and accompanying aggression, and she prescribed a medication also prescribed for schizophrenia. Within weeks Michael gained some internal calm for the first time in years. Within months his symptoms subsided enough to allow him to learn, work on scout badges, and achieve modest successes.

Simultaneously, Michelle began experiencing disturbingly bizarre moments. For weeks at a time she hid her feces wrapped in paper towels inside of drawers. We would find these later by the undeniable odor. When questioned, she was as confused and troubled by this as we were. At night she was terrified by visions of ghastly, bloody persons appearing in her room. Michelle could not concentrate on her schoolwork and regressed in her abilities. She heard ethereal, tormenting voices telling her she must die. In a moment unknown to us, she taped her Last Will and Testament to the bottom of her bed frame. The voices taunted her, and she could not make them stop. She begged me to stay close to her. During these years I started each homeschooling day with a Bible reading and devotional lesson as much for myself as for the children. I needed help.[5]

You Are Not Alone

At just the right time Concordia Seminary in Saint Louis hosted a small conference on mental illness. I drove well over an hour to attend. As I pulled into the long driveway of the seminary campus, the sign *You Are Not Alone* brought unexpected tears. The thought

---

5   As young adults, Michael and Michelle now share their stories with the hope that others who witness or experience such early signs will seek immediate help.

that, at last, someone might understand my children gave me enough courage to park my car and enter the event.

I had arrived early, so I explored the room. One booth featured a bullet-point list of warning signs for severe mental illness. Not ready to read them, I pocketed the flier and moved along the row of vendors, stopping to pick up a brochure from the First Contact Clinic at Washington University in Saint Louis. Further down, an older woman introduced herself from NAMI, the National Alliance for the Mentally Ill, and I learned gratefully that she lived just minutes from me.

Only after finding a seat did I dare to read that bullet-point list of symptoms. The list was far too familiar. Soon I could no longer look up as tears spilled from my eyes. Between the two children we had every symptom in our home:

- Difficulties concentrating
- Academic regression
- Extreme highs and lows
- Excessive fears or worries
- Dramatic or odd changes in behavior
- Confused thinking
- Strange or paranoid thoughts (delusions)
- Seeing or hearing things that are not real (hallucinations)
- Defiance of authority, theft, and/or vandalism
- Inability to cope with daily problems and activities
- Frequent tantrums or outbursts of anger
- Persistent nightmares
- Speaking of death or dying

As I fought my tears, the seminar leader began the session. She shared many insights, but as I settled into her story, this one especially impacted me: the mentally ill need someone they trust to verify what is (and is not) reality. This made sense. Suddenly I knew my role. Then her husband, a pastor, spoke to us, beginning with this stinging reminder: "If you love someone with mental illness, you are no better than that person. We are here to love and serve each other." He proclaimed mercy, forgiveness, and hope for us all in Jesus Christ alone. Here was a pastor bringing the Gospel to bear upon my own transgressions with hope for my children and for me.

That day my heart calmed, my fears stilled, and my courage grew. Life under the cross would continue for us, as for everyone, but the Lord would be with us. Mental illness was no longer an amorphous, unspoken fear; instead, it was something these people had encountered in their families too. I became fortified to serve my children, to understand them better, and to obtain the best care we could find. "For as we share abundantly in Christ's sufferings, so through Christ we share abundantly in comfort too."[6]

I left that seminar equipped with what I needed to know: mental illness was undeniably upon us. I left with a brochure that would eventually lead us to expert help from a Washington University doctor, a published researcher in schizophrenia, who evaluated and diagnosed both of my children and who guides us to this day. I left with the knowledge that I would return often to the cross of Christ through Word and Sacrament for hope and help, fortification and forgiveness. Armed for the battle, a restful strength was mine.

> To pastures green, Lord, safely guide,
>   To restful waters lead me;
> Your table well for me provide,
>   Your wounded hand now feed me.
> Though weary, sinful, sick, and weak,
> Refuge in You alone I seek,
>   To share Your cup of healing.[7]

TODAY AND TOMORROW

Schizophrenia comes with a life expectancy twenty-five years shorter than average. On Ash Wednesday this year, I watched

---

6   2 Corinthians 1:5
7   "Lord Jesus Christ, Life-Giving Bread" (stanza 2) by Johann Rist, tr. Arthur T. Russell.

both of my adult children approach the altar to receive ashes. As I witnessed our pastor make the sign of the cross upon my children's foreheads, I heard the truth that remains for us all: "Remember that 'you are dust, and to dust you shall return.'"[8] Our children's mental and physical fragility serve to remind me of their ongoing spiritual need. I am grateful that both children continue to live with us. We pray with them nightly, and they attend church with us every Sunday. Both children also commune and attend adult Bible class with us.

Following a recent bout of severe hallucinations, Michael felt his own human weakness. We contacted his doctor to cover medical needs. Michael sensed not only the weakness of his flesh but also the temptations of the world and the wiles of the devil. He confided to me quietly, "I need to go to church and hear Pastor's good Gospel."

THE MERCY OF OUR GOOD SHEPHERD

Many years ago when we checked "no" to our ability to handle mental illness, we were right. We never could have handled this alone. Thanks be to God, we are not alone. No matter the trials, no matter the waves and winds of our children's frailties and our own, our Lord gives us strength in our weakness. Our struggles are temporal, but the "steadfast love of the LORD never ceases; His mercies never come to an end."[9]

> Be still, my soul; the hour is hast'ning on
>   When we shall be forever with the Lord,
> When disappointment, grief, and fear are gone,
>   Sorrow forgot, love's purest joys restored.
> Be still, my soul; when change and tears are past,
> All safe and blessed we shall meet at last.[10]

---

8   Genesis 3:19
9   Lamentations 3:22
10   "Be Still My Soul" (stanza 4) by Catharina Amalia Dorothea von Schlegel, tr. Jane L. Borthwick.

Our protective Shepherd will strengthen us to bear any cross we have been given. His Word promises this.[11] Again and again, as He does for my children, so our Lord does for me. Day by day, moment by moment, my Good Shepherd leads me beside still waters and into the comforting mercy of His eternal love.

---

11   Psalm 10:17, 1 Peter 5:10, Ephesians 6:16, and Isaiah 41:10, my daughter's beloved confirmation verse.

CHAPTER FIVE

I Am Herod
by Katie Schuermann

"He restores my soul."
Psalm 23:3

"Are you ready, Eden?"

I looked at Liza, my friend in good times and in bad. She was buttoned up to her chin in a bright blue coat—cheerful in shade, just like her—and a few stray, gray-streaked curls sprang out from underneath her green stocking cap. A pair of red-framed eyeglasses sat above the homemade scarf that was wrapped no fewer than three times around her face. The January wind could try as it might, but it was no match for Liza's yarn fortress.

"It's time," she said. I felt her encouraging smile more than saw it.

I took a deep breath, picked up the sign that had been leaning against my knees, and followed my friend out into the busy street. Thousands and thousands of people in parkas and snow boots were already trudging up Constitution Avenue, some waving banners, some pushing strollers, and some gripping rosaries. A group of college students to my left immediately erupted into a unison chant: "Hey, hey! Ho, ho! Roe v. Wade has got to go! Hey, hey—"

Liza grabbed my arm protectively and pulled me around a cluster of praying nuns and through a chatty youth group wearing matching sweatshirts to a quieter corner of the procession.

"God bless those kids," her voice reverberated from somewhere within her scarf mountain, "but cheers fall a bit flat on the ears today, don't you think?"

I knew what she was doing, and I loved her for it. I settled into step beside her and ventured a quick peek over my sign. A pro-life group walking ahead of us sang a hymn in four-part harmony. A teenage boy toward the back of the pack stopped and knelt on one knee in the middle of the street to tie his shoe. I caught a glimpse of the slogan on his sign: "Abortion stops a beating heart."

You stopped a beating heart.

I grimaced. Despite the cold, my hands broke into a sweat.

You stopped your baby's heart.

My mouth went dry. The voice was only in my head, but I spoke aloud to it anyway. "'There is therefore now no condemnation for those who are in Christ Jesus.'"[1]

Liza didn't bat an eye at my self-talk. She knew what I was doing. She was the one who had taught me to do it. "Replace the negative voice with a positive one," she had said during one of our sessions.

My pastor had taken Liza's counsel one step further. "Replace Satan's voice with God's."

"How?"

"Memorize God's Word and speak it aloud. Recite the creeds. Pray. Sing hymns. Drown out Satan's chiding with holy truth."

I sniffed at the devil and started to sing:

> O little flock, fear not the foe
> Who madly seeks your overthrow;
>   Dread not his rage and pow'r.
> And though your courage sometimes faints,
> His seeming triumph o'er God's saints
>   Lasts but a little hour.[2]

---

1   Romans 8:1
2   "O Little Flock, Fear Not the Foe" (stanza 1) by Jacob Fabricius, tr. Catherine Winkworth.

Before I could start in on stanza two, something hit me hard at the back of my knees.

"Charlie! Watch where you're going!"

I turned in time to see a mother grabbing a young boy by the hand and yanking him back to her side.

"You ran right into this nice woman, Charlie," the mother reprimanded.

You're not nice.

The woman stopped in the middle of the march like a rock in a stream. Rivulets of people continued to flow around us. "Apologize to the nice woman at once."

She wouldn't ask her son to apologize if she knew what you'd done.

I swallowed. I couldn't look at the mother or the boy. I hid my sign at my side.

"Say you're sorry, Charlie."

The boy hid his face against his mother's coat. "Sorry," I heard him whisper.

"I'm sure it was an accident," I mumbled, turning around and moving forward, away from the little boy, away from his fear, away from my pain.

Liza's red glasses were turned my way.

"I'm fine," I murmured. "Just keep walking." I sang even louder:

> Be of good cheer; your cause belongs
> To Him who can avenge your wrongs;
> Leave it to Him, our Lord—[3]

"Eden," Liza interrupted, "close your eyes."

"What? Why?"

"Just do it."

I did, even as Liza continued to pull me forward. "What is it?"

---

[3] "O Little Flock, Fear Not the Foe" (stanza 2) by Jacob Fabricius, tr. Catherine Winkworth.

"Those organizations that show images of aborted babies are here again," Liza spoke, her voice tight. "They're projecting pictures on a jumbo screen ahead."

I squeezed my eyes shut.

Afraid to look at your child? Afraid to see what you've done?

"They're showing these to the wrong crowd," Liza sighed near my ear, her irritation audible. "I mean, really. C'mon, people. At a pro-life march? How does this help the situation?"

"People need to know," I said.

"All of us here already know. This is not a crowd of the ignorant, Eden. And nothing about these images encourages hurting women to have conversations with the pro-life community." She grumbled purposefully, "Hold tight. We're almost past."

Fifty more feet or so ahead, I opened my eyes and stretched my shoulders. A stranger fell in step beside me, and I turned to my right to look into a kind, lined face.

"Thank you for being here," the woman said, reaching a sisterly arm around my shoulders. She nodded significantly at my sign.

My sign. I had completely forgotten I was holding it. It read, "I regret my abortion." I felt my cheeks flush with a sudden heat.

"May I ask you a question?" the woman continued.

I was mortified, but I was here for this very thing. To be asked questions. To answer them. To tell people the truth. "Yes."

"What can I do? You know, how can I care for you, for women who regret their abortions? My sister aborted her child twenty years ago. I want to help her."

"Pray for her."

"I do."

"Pray for the doctor and nurses who performed the abortion."

"Okay."

"Help other women who are pregnant. Your sister and I—our abortions will always be with us. We don't want that for anyone else."

Murderer.

I swallowed.

"And never tell your sister, 'It's okay.'" I noticed that my voice had raised in pitch. I took a deep breath, trying to calm down. "My baby was alive in my womb, and I had her killed. Murder is murder. It's not okay, and Satan knows it and uses it against me and your sister every day. So never lie to her. That will not help her."

"What will help her?"

"The truth. The truth that even women who abort their children are forgiven by God."

Did God really say—? [4]

Oh, yes, He did!

"'If anyone does sin,'" I recited aloud, as much for my sake as for the woman's, "'we have an advocate with the Father, Jesus Christ the righteous. He is the propitiation for our sins, and not for ours only but also for the sins of the whole world.'"[5]

Pastor had encouraged me to memorize those verses from chapter 2 of 1 John. Actually, he had suggested I commit the entire chapter to memory.

"Our 'sins are forgiven for His name's sake,'"[6] I added.

Are you sure?

Yes!

"'If we confess our sins, He is faithful and just to forgive us our sins and to cleanse us from all unrighteousness.'"[7]

After the woman thanked me and rejoined her fellow marchers, Liza linked her arm in mine and squeezed. "Preach it, sister."

"That was hard," I breathed.

"You and I aren't here today for the easy things in life."

---

4   Genesis 3:1
5   1 John 2:1–2
6   1 John 2:12
7   1 John 1:9

We were now turning right onto First Street. The stately Supreme Court building stood guard over the march to our left, and the frozen lawn of the Capitol grounds sprawled on our right.

"This is us," Liza said, nodding toward a micro-cluster of people encircling a microphone at the foot of the Supreme Court steps. The marching mass behind us threatened to keep pushing us forward, so we cut across the pressing crowd to claim a small piece of stability on the sidewalk.

"Hang here for a minute," Liza said, disappearing behind a line of downy coats.

Do you really believe—?

I didn't have time for this. Not now. I was about to do one of the hardest things I had ever done in my life, and Satan was making a powerful play for my peace, my soul. I stared at the ground and sang:

> As true as God's own Word is true,
> Not earth nor hell's satanic crew
>   Against us shall prevail.
> Their might? A joke, a mere facade!
> God is with us and we with God—
>   Our vict'ry cannot fail.[8]

Liza rejoined me on the sidewalk and held out her hand. "Here, give me your sign."

A wave of anxiety washed over me. The insides of my elbows began to itch under my winter clothes. If I could have gotten at them with my fingernails, I would have. Instead, I stared helplessly at my gloved hands.

Nothing was lost on Liza.

"You're up first, honey," she prodded. She began unwrapping her scarf with her free hand and nodded over her shoulder toward the microphone. "Go on. I'll go after you, okay?"

---

8   "O Little Flock, Fear Not the Foe" (stanza 3) by Jacob Fabricius, tr. Catherine Winkworth.

I locked my shaking hands under my armpits, took a deep breath, and stomped the cold out of my toes. This is why I had traveled to our nation's capital during the coldest month of the year. This is why I had marched up that hill with hundreds of thousands of strangers. And this microphone was my opportunity to—

You can't ever make right what you did.

—help all of those helpless children and scared mothers.

There is nothing you can do—

I can tell everyone the truth.

I stepped before the microphone and looked out over a sea of inquiring eyes, some of them friendly, many of them sad. Thousands of people beyond were still marching noisily down First Street, chanting and singing and praying and holding signs and waving bright blue and red and green and gold banners overhead. The noisy sight calmed me, for colors have always reminded me of God's presence. Stained-glass windows, altar paraments, and here, amidst the noisy chaos of like-minded strangers, the bold logos of various religious orders and pro-life organizations offered colorful support.

I took a deep, shaky breath.

"My name is Eden," I began, my confession crystalizing in the cold air before me, "and I regret my abortion."

Murderer.

"I was twenty-three when my boyfriend drove me to Planned Parenthood." I searched the back of the crowd for Liza. Her green hat bobbed encouragingly. I took another breath. "I felt anxious in the waiting room. In fact, I grew so agitated that the nurse sent me home with a two-day supply of Valium and an appointment card for the next day the abortion doctor would be in town. I often wonder why no one at the clinic suggested to me that maybe my anxiety was an indication that I didn't really want to abort my baby."

A woman standing before me started to cry.

"Two days later, my boyfriend drove me back. There were so many women in the waiting room that day—women with their mothers, their friends, their husbands, some of them alone—but all of them there for the same reason as me. There is comfort in numbers. I felt no shame, no guilt, with so many other women there for the same thing.

"They called us back five at a time to show us a video of the type of procedure we were going to have. I was at nine weeks, so I was grouped with all of the women having a suction abortion. I couldn't watch the video. I panicked. I told the nurse that if I watched it, I would never be able to go through with it. So she talked me through the procedure, instead, and showed me where to sign on the papers.

"Then, we were individually called back to private rooms. Mine was tiny, no bigger than a closet, with two doors on either side of a bed—one for me to use and the other for the doctor. I laid on the bed in the middle of the room, and two nurses stood nearby—one at a sink and the other at a counter along the wall. I realized later that the nurse at the counter was there to piece my baby's parts back together to make sure the doctor had gotten everything."

The crying woman held a tissue to her mouth.

"I was awake for the entire procedure. It hurt so bad. I was crying out in pain, but no one in the room said a word to me, except when the doctor said, 'We're done,' at the end. A nurse led me out to a waiting room with all of the other women. They offered orange juice and cookies to those of us who felt 'weak,' while the weakest of us all—the babies—were disposed of by the medical staff. From start to finish, I was in Planned Parenthood for only thirty minutes."

I looked at the clamorous crowd gathered in the street—the chanting college students, the praying nuns, the singing church groups—most of whom could not hear a single word of my confession, but if my story could help even one person at this march, encourage one grieving mother, or bend the resolve of one abortion-minded woman, then something good would have come from this awful mess.

"My pastor tells me the truth, that murder is a sin—"

Murderer.

"But it is a sin for which Jesus died. I cling to the fact that I put on Christ in my Baptism.[9] His righteousness is made mine. My sins are washed away in the flood of His blood, and I am forgiven even of murder."

The woman in front of me nodded, wiping at her eyes.

"I often think about Christ's prayer on the cross: 'Father, forgive them, for they know not what they do.'[10] I didn't really know what I was doing all those years ago at Planned Parenthood, and still Jesus prays for me. I cling to His abundant mercy. I cling to His Holy Absolution, to the words of forgiveness that loose me from the bondage of my sin.[11] I cling in faith to Christ's Holy Supper, to His 'blood of the covenant, which is poured out for many'—for me—'for the forgiveness of sins.'"[12]

Liza was grinning at me from under that colorful, comforting green hat. Her smile always surprised me. So much joy even amidst so much pain and sadness. She trusted in God's mercy. So did I.

"I am Herod," I confessed, the truth catching in my throat. "I killed an innocent child—"

Murderer.

"But God forgives me."

I swallowed. I was almost done. Just one more true thing to say.

"God forgives me, and His forgiveness restores my soul."

> Come, Holy Ghost, Creator blest,
> And make our hearts Your place of rest;
>> Come with Your grace and heav'nly aid,
>> And fill the hearts which You have made.

---

9   Galatians 3:27
10   Luke 23:34
11   John 20:19–23
12   Matthew 26:28

Anoint and cheer our much-soiled face
With the abundance of Your grace.
    Keep far our foes; give peace at home;
    Where You guide us, no ill can come.

Drive far away our wily foe,
And Your abiding peace bestow;
    With You as our protecting guide,
    No evil can with us abide.[13]

---

13   "Come, Holy Ghost, Creator Blest" attr. Rabanus Maurus; (stanzas 1, 5) tr.
      Edward Caswall, (stanza 3) tr. John Cosin.

CHAPTER SIX

Getting Past Your Past

by Cheryl Magness

"He leads me in paths of righteousness for His name's sake."
Psalm 23:3

Almost twenty-five years ago, I sat by my father's deathbed, my firstborn on my lap, a Father's Day card in my hands. In the card was a letter I had written to my father about the Jesus I had come to know, the Jesus he and I had never talked about. I had planned to mail the card but, in light of his deteriorating condition, had come to him in person. Now, sitting by his bedside, I could not bring myself to read him the letter. I did not remember ever seeing my father in church except on my wedding day, but I knew that he was baptized. As he lay silent, his eyes closed, I leaned over and whispered in his ear, "Jesus loves you, Daddy. He will take care of you." My father nodded. At his funeral, I slipped the card in his casket.

I do not remember attending church or praying with my parents as a child. I longed to go to church and sometimes watched worship services on television while communing my dolls. I read my mom's self-help and power-of-positive-thinking books, but one look at my home life belied the promise that all one needed to find peace was the proper frame of mind.

I was born about a year-and-a-half after my parents were married, the second marriage for both. My father, recently widowed, had four children, all but one of whom were grown; my mother, divorced from an abusive first husband, had six. Neither of them was equipped for the task they had undertaken of trying to blend two families still reeling from the effects of death and divorce. As my father slipped deeper into alcoholism, my mother found it easier to drink with him than not.

My predominant memories of the first ten years of my life involve a lot of yelling and swearing and, on occasion, physical displays of anger; my father passing out at the dining room table or cursing loudly outside as he worked on our cars; embarrassment at bringing friends over because I did not know what scene might transpire; and insufficient supervision of children. Once, when I was only five or six, one of my sisters, babysitting me at the time, took me to a garishly-decorated apartment. When I described it to her years later, she was horrified. "Cheryl, I took you there?" she said. "I'm sorry." We had visited a drug dealer.

I learned during my childhood to stay out of the way so as not to upset whatever small amount of peace there was. I read a lot, both to keep busy and to shut out my surroundings and mentally escape. Yet despite the volatile environment, I never doubted my parents' love for me, nor did I worry about being properly fed and clothed. And even though we did not attend church that I recall, my parents had seen fit when I was a baby to have me baptized in the name of the Triune God, and for that I will always be grateful.

"He saved us, not because of works done by us in righteousness, but according to His own mercy, by the washing of regeneration and renewal of the Holy Spirit."[1]

A few years ago, I read *Hillbilly Elegy*,[2] J. D. Vance's memoir about

---

1   Titus 3:5
2   J. D. Vance, *Hillbilly Elegy: A Memoir of a Family and Culture in Crisis* (New York: HarperCollins, 2016).

the difficulty of getting past a dysfunctional upbringing in order to follow a different path. The book rang true, and not just because I have hillbilly roots. Vance describes something called the ACE score for Adverse Childhood Experiences.[3] The higher the ACE score, the more likely one is to suffer negative physical, mental, and emotional consequences in adulthood stemming from childhood.

It is a concept that should not be surprising to Christians. The sins of parents have been visited upon children ever since our first parents decided to follow their own path rather than God's. The Bible is brimming with stories of sin-riddled, dysfunctional families—stories that painfully demonstrate the ripple effect of sin, from Adam and Eve,[4] to Cain and Abel,[5] to Jacob and Esau,[6] to Joseph and his brothers.[7] That is just in Genesis alone!

> **"For I the LORD your God am a jealous God,**
> **visiting the iniquity of the fathers on the**
> **children to the third and the fourth generation**
> **of those who hate Me . . ."[8]**

Most of us do not have to look very far to see that ripple effect up close. It would take an entire book to chronicle the dysfunction in my own family, but nowhere is it so apparent as in the divorce rate of my ten siblings, of whom only two have never been divorced. My husband, who also comes from an unchurched, dysfunctional background, is the only one of the four children in his family to have never been divorced. That we have remained married to each other for over thirty-one years is a victory against the odds.

It is not our victory, though; it is God's. For years, my husband and I have strived to create a Christian family culture

---

3   "Adverse Childhood Experiences," *Substance Abuse and Mental Health Services Administration.* https://www.samhsa.gov/capt/practicing-effective-prevention/prevention-behavioral-health/adverse-childhood-experiences (accessed May 5, 2018).

4   Genesis 3

5   Genesis 4:8–16

6   Genesis 27

7   Genesis 37

8   Exodus 20:5

in our own home when we did not grow up with one. Yet I know full well that the life we have is not our achievement, but the gift of a gracious God. In the beginning, we had no idea what we were doing, but as I look back from the perspective of having almost completed our child-rearing years, I can see some of the things that made a difference.

> **"For by grace you have been saved through faith.**
> **And this is not your own doing; it is the gift of**
> **God, not a result of works, so that**
> **no one may boast."**[9]

Before my husband and I had our first child, in what I consider to be one of the miracles of our life together, he was offered a position as a church musician. It was not something he planned to do—he was working freelance, playing lounge piano and teaching at a local college—but when the position became available at the church we were attending, he was asked to take it. I would like to think that even without his becoming a church worker, we would have nevertheless been faithful in our church attendance since we were already going regularly, but I have no way of knowing.

I do know that when we told my mother-in-law that we could not spend all of Christmas Eve with the family because we were going to church, her response was that we were ruining everyone's Christmas. Would we have stood as strong against her displeasure if we had not *had* to be at church? Again, I do not know, but I do know it was not easy to be seen as the enemy simply because we were going to church.

> **"Do not be surprised, brothers,**
> **that the world hates you."**[10]

I cannot be sure what would have happened if our life had gone differently, but I am thankful that the Lord led us in the path

---

9   Ephesians 2:8–9
10   1 John 3:13

He did, because that path has led us to church every week—and then some—for over thirty years. Our children have never known anything else but that church is where Jesus is.

Not only is church where Jesus is; it is where other Christians are. For my husband and me, church provided an endless supply of faithful Christian parents to whom we could look as examples. From them we learned that rearing children in the faith means praying with them, having family devotions, reading the Bible together, studying the teachings of the Church, and talking about God—not just occasionally, but all the time.

I am convinced, however, that more than anything, regular church attendance taught us to be Christian parents. Going to church week in and week out, my husband and I were ourselves formed in the faith as we heard God's Word in the liturgy and preaching and responded to that Word in the hymns and prayers of the Church. As that faith became more a part of us, it inevitably became a part of our home.

Prayer was not something we had to try to do; it was a natural outgrowth of our daily lives. When sins were committed and commandments broken, we followed a biblical pattern of repentance and forgiveness, even to the point of reciting the commandment in question and discussing how it had been broken. When difficult questions arose, we turned to God's Word for answers. One of the greatest joys of my life today is when one of my children reminds me to pray, directs me to God's Word, or otherwise models the living out of the faith. It is a blessing beyond compare, indeed a microcosm of the Church, to realize that your children are also your brothers and sisters in Christ, and to see the faith you have tried to share with them coming back to you.

**"Faith comes from hearing,
and hearing through the word of Christ."**[11]

Probably the most influential example for us as Christian parents was the senior pastor and his wife at the first church my husband

---

11   Romans 10:17

served full-time. In their guest bathroom was a sign that read, "While we're busy giving our children all the things we didn't have, let's not forget to give them all the things we had." The sign reflected their approach to parenting, and we spent many hours in their home learning what that entailed.

One of the most important lessons we learned from this couple was the centrality of mealtime to the family's life together. It was not something I grew up experiencing. My primary memory of mealtimes is of people eating in isolation, grabbing food on their own schedules, or eating on folding trays in front of the television. I had an aunt who insisted, when she came to visit, not only that we eat together at the table but that we pray before eating. I loved it when Aunt Lou visited.

My husband's family ate together but did not pray together. From our pastor, we learned to make the family meal an occasion for study, fellowship, and prayer, not purely for physical sustenance but for spiritual and emotional sustenance as well. It is a practice we have kept to this day, one that imitates on a small scale the coming together of the whole Body of Christ in the liturgy of the Lord's Supper.

> **"And they devoted themselves to the apostles'**
> **teaching and the fellowship, to the breaking**
> **of bread and the prayers."**[12]

When you have grown up in a dysfunctional environment, it is easy to look to that environment as the cause of all your personal problems and failings. In my case, the temptation is great for me to blame my past for a host of personal weaknesses that have set the stage for poor decisions over the years: my desire to be in control, my tendency toward perfectionism, my excessive concern about what others think, my need for approval, my shrinking from conflict, and my propensity for worry and anxiety. Yet the truth is that I am a sinner and still would be even if my childhood

---

12   Acts 2:42

had been healthier. Spending my days pointing to my upbringing as the source of my difficulties does not help me rehabilitate those difficulties, nor does it overcome the essential problem of sin.

"None is righteous, no, not one."[13]

For most of the last fifteen years of her life, my mother lived with me. It was not easy to have her in my house, but it was extremely easy to blame her for my own struggles with impatience, anger, resentment, and hurt when I deemed her own behavior unacceptable.

Yet I had no one to blame but myself. Sin is never the fault of another and always the fault of the sinner. God's Word is clear on how we are to treat our parents, even when they sin against us. In fact, as noted by St. Paul, it is the only command with a promise attached to it: "Honor your father and mother . . . that it may go well with you and that you may live long in the land."[14] Of the Fourth Commandment, Martin Luther wrote:

> Learn, therefore, what is the honor towards parents that this commandment requires. (a) They must be held in distinction and esteem above all things, as the most precious treasure on earth. (b) In our words we must speak modestly toward them (Proverbs 15:1). Do not address them roughly, haughtily, and defiantly. But yield to them and be silent, even though they go too far.[15]

I was not always silent when my mom went "too far."

It is not necessarily wrong to consider how the things that have happened to us have shaped us and to use that knowledge to become healthier, better-functioning people. Ultimately, though, our sinful nature is something we are born with, and our actions are our own responsibility. There is no one else to blame. The

---

13   Romans 3:10
14   Ephesians 6:2–3
15   From *Concordia: The Lutheran Confessions* © 2007 Concordia Publishing House. Used with permission. www.cph.org.

sooner we acknowledge that, and repent, the sooner we can receive God's forgiveness and, in turn, give it to others.

"If we confess our sins, He is faithful and just
to forgive us our sins and to cleanse us
from all unrighteousness."[16]

Psalm 37 reminds us that righteousness comes from God, not from ourselves: "Commit your way to the LORD; trust in Him, and He will act. He will bring forth your righteousness as the light, and your justice as the noonday."[17] In the area of childrearing, we can do everything "right" and still our children will sin, stumble, fall, perhaps even reject the faith they have been taught.

Meanwhile, He mercifully calls to Himself wandering sheep who were not brought up to know His voice, and yet they hear His voice and come. The question of why some reject the faith they were given and others grasp at a faith they were not taught will always be a mystery to us this side of heaven. Our job is not to answer the question of why, but to trust and pray, knowing that our Good Shepherd does not give up on His sheep.[18]

". . . but showing steadfast love to thousands
of those who love Me and keep
My commandments."[19]

Twenty-two years after I sat at my father's deathbed, I repeated the scene at my mother's deathbed. This time, instead of my oldest child sitting on my lap, my youngest sat by my side. In fact, he not only sat by my side, he spent hours alone with his grandmother, holding her hand, praying with her, singing to her, and telling her that Jesus loved her.

---

16   1 John 1:9
17   Psalm 37:5–6
18   John 10:14
19   Exodus 20:6

It was a message my mother desperately needed to hear. She had been abandoned in childhood by her parents, left to be raised by relatives, and married to two men who did not love her as Christ loved the Church. As a young woman, she was baptized at the encouragement of friends but then spent many years away from her baptismal faith. In her late forties, she returned to the Church, but she never stopped struggling with guilt, doubt, and uncertainty about her worthiness before God. I wish she could have left this life with more peace than she did.

Looking through her Bible after she died, I came upon Psalm 27, where she had underlined verse 10: "For my father and my mother have forsaken me, but the LORD will take me in." I had the words engraved on her tombstone.

This is a message we all need to hear, because no matter who we are or how we were raised, our parents will in one way or another let us down, as will the rest of our family, our friends, our church, even our pastors. But there is One who will not forsake us, even as, in our sinfulness, we deserve to be forsaken. Not only will He not forsake us, He will not forsake our children, or our grandchildren, or any He has claimed for His own: "If we are faithless, He remains faithful—for He cannot deny Himself."[20]

> I heard the voice of Jesus say,
>   "I am this dark world's light.
> Look unto Me; thy morn shall rise
>   And all thy day be bright."
> I looked to Jesus, and I found
>   In Him my star, my sun;
> And in that light of life I'll walk
>   Till trav'ling days are done.[21]

---

20   2 Timothy 2:13
21   "I Heard the Voice of Jesus Say" (stanza 3) by Horatius Bonar.

CHAPTER SEVEN

Incompatible with Life

by Magdalena Schultz

"Even though I walk through the valley of the shadow of death,
I will fear no evil."

Psalm 23:4

I would love to say that I am handling the situation well. I would love to say that I never burst out in anger and disappointment. Sure, I can control myself in public and put on that "brave face" and thank everyone for their kind words and prayers, and I genuinely am grateful; however, I am also a poor miserable sinner. The question of "Why me?" all too often escapes my lips. So many children are born healthy every day. Why is my child the exception? What did I do wrong?

In May of 2017, Christian and I celebrated our wedding. Three months after that, we found out we were parents. Then, in a dimly-lit examination room halfway through our second trimester, we learned that our little child was sick. The crucial moments following this news forced us to grow up all too quickly. At twenty-four years old, neither of us feels old enough to be having a child, let alone one with severe health difficulties.

Of all of the bewildering medical information dumped on us that day, the worst remains the diagnosis that our baby is "incompatible with life." Up until those three words, I had understood the gravity of a double cleft lip as well as the severity of brain, heart, and esophagus deformities; even the possible diagnoses of chromosomal abnormality and trisomy did not terrify me half as much as those three words, which seemed absent of all hope. Offering us the most frequently chosen option, the fetal cardiologist followed his diagnosis by suggesting a "therapeutic termination of pregnancy." After all, why put off the inevitable miscarriage or stillbirth? Why not just erase all of this and try again? Even if our child made it to term and survived birth, how would our baby's "quality of life" ever be worth all of the hardship?

Oh, how the evil one tempts us! He knows exactly when and where we are the most vulnerable. Our sinful nature is already inclined to usurp the order of creation, to place ourselves in the position of Creator, especially concerning children.

In calm and collected words, the doctor presented us with the option of placing our own emotional comfort over the inconveniences that our child would surely cause. Thankfully, God's children are never left alone to face the devil. With strength and clarity that could have come only from our Lord, I saw through our difficult predicament and realized that my baby needed me—his mother—more than ever. After all, what had I been doing up until this point but protecting and nourishing my child? By rejecting the selfish option, I would continue supporting this little one entrusted to my care, and yet from now on, my vocation would entail more than merely taking the right prenatal vitamins and avoiding some foods. I, like every mother before me, was being called to show the world the great worth and preciousness of the very life growing inside of me.

I quickly grew frustrated with how vaguely this doctor discussed the disturbing problems plaguing my child. How could someone come in, look at some grainy pictures, hypothesize about the condition of our child, and then tell us death was the best option? With no actual confirmation that there was a chromosomal issue and with four more months until my due date, I would not give up hope. I needed a second opinion, and if that was not enough, I wanted a third. I wanted a doctor who would seek to heal, not kill. While our child might have serious health issues, it was now up to us as parents to make sure we found the best treatment and care. After all, someone who is clearly already alive could not possibly be incompatible with life.

I was so thankful that Christian and I had already discussed our concerns surrounding genetic testing at the beginning of our pregnancy. We originally declined early testing, for no test result could ever change our respect for life or convince us to abort our child. Now, faced with the imminent health challenges projected by the doctor, we chose the least dangerous test offered to our child: a noninvasive blood screening that would either confirm or dismiss the doctor's diagnosis of a chromosomal trisomy while also opening the door for referrals to other doctors.

Our last stop at the nurses' desk that day gave us the opportunity to inquire if the baby's sex had been identified during the echocardiogram. With the doctor's words "miscarriage" and "likely stillbirth" still ringing in our ears, we had come to the quick realization that we wanted this little bit of information. If our time together as a family would be shorter than expected, then we wanted to get to know our child now as best we could. We drove home that day with the happy news that we have a son, and we threw ourselves into the joyful, life-affirming parental task of naming him.

Always with their meanings in mind, Christian and I worked through list after list of family, historical, and biblical names before finally finding and choosing Noah. The account of the flood and the ark in the Book of Genesis[1] certainly influenced our decision—it evokes images of safety and God's never-ending faithfulness to His children—but the actual meaning of Noah, *rest* or *comfort*, made the name even more perfect.

Noah's middle names came a bit more easily. We discovered and chose Laurence, meaning *laurel-crowned*, because of an Epistle reading one Sunday morning. The apostle Paul writes at the very end of his first letter to the Corinthians how runners receive a perishable laurel crown at the end of a race, yet we Christians will receive an imperishable wreath from our faithful

---

1   Genesis 6:11—8:22

Father in heaven once we complete our earthly race.[2] Christian and I were also inspired by St. Laurence, a deacon in third-century Rome, whose actions proclaimed the love of God to the world. As church tradition holds, the Emperor Valerian charged Laurence to give to him the vast riches of the Church. Laurence followed this order and gathered the widows, the poor, the weak, the ill, and the orphans of the city and brought them before the emperor, presenting them as the true treasure of the Church.

We also proudly passed on to Noah the name of his father, Christian, as a clear reminder of his salvation in Christ. Our son's full name, Noah Laurence Christian, confesses our belief to each other and to the world that God will give our son peace and rest. Though he is vulnerable and weak, he remains the true treasure of the Church.

The task of naming our son led us directly to the comforting realization that God is Noah's true Father, and that being parents to this little life is a gift—a privilege—from Him. We are new at this vocation, but we have quickly learned that we have no control over how long Noah will remain with us before or after birth. Whether it is ten seconds, ten days, or ten years, we cherish every little kick and hiccup we feel, and Lord willing, we look forward to meeting him face-to-face in a few short weeks.

Even our kind OB/GYN gently reminded us that parents never know how long their children will live. This is a universal reality of parenthood, and the length of a child's life does not determine the value of that life. With all of this in mind, our days have become much more intentional, for we are given one day at a time for a reason. The words recorded in the Gospel of Matthew have taken on new meaning for us and our little one, for who "by being anxious can add a single hour to his span of life?"[3] I frequently think back to that question of the quality of little Noah's life, and amazingly, I can already show how, while still in the womb, he has touched so many hearts—most especially mine. What he has taught me about the preciousness of life, family, and

---

2   1 Corinthians 9:24–25
3   Matthew 6:27

parenting has immeasurable worth, and I cannot imagine my life without him.

As it so often turns out in the Christian life, our greatest frustrations become our greatest blessings. With no specific cause to blame, the truth of our sinful nature becomes unavoidably clear. The fall of man and the entrance of sin and death into the world makes all of us incompatible with life,[4] and yet our Heavenly Father has already resolved this plight. By sending His own dearly beloved Son to restore His earthly creation and grant us the promise of eternal life, the threats and troubles of this world have no lasting hold on us. Keeping all of this in mind during the good days and the bad becomes a daily exercise of faith. Not the kind of faith that gets easier over time, but the kind that must be repeated anew each day as if from the beginning. Thankfully, God gives us only one day at a time, and this allows us to give our struggles and vocations the care they require.

With every change in life comes a time of transition, and in our case, Christian and I have had a very abrupt introduction into parenthood. Not only is pregnancy in itself a completely new world for both of us, but ours has taken a turn that can no longer be compared with those of our pregnant siblings and friends. This has certainly been isolating. Instead of preparing a nursery and taking birthing classes, we are commuting to the children's hospital two hours away for extensive testing and meetings. We have not read any parenting books, and yet we are acquiring an entirely new lexicon of medical vocabulary and can explain heaps of complicated physical conditions. I often wish that our decisions could be as simple as choosing which stroller we want. Discontentment and frustration creep in too often. Even jealousy emerges occasionally, yet all of these base emotions remind me again and again of my great need for a Savior. They chase me back to repentance of my sins and the comforting forgiveness earned for me by Christ on the cross.

Just as St. Peter comforted the exiles of the early Christian church, his words still bring great comfort to those of us who

---

4   Genesis 3

realize we ought "not be surprised at the fiery trial when it comes upon you to test you, as though something strange were happening to you. But rejoice insofar as you share Christ's sufferings, that you may also rejoice and be glad when His glory is revealed."[5] When faced with the possibility of an early death for our son, we are reminded in His Word that Christ's glory over death remains the only true comfort in our moments of darkest despair. Clinging to the foot of the cross like my own namesake, Mary Magdalene,[6] I have learned again and again what a great miracle Christ's love for us is.

Even still, my little mind struggles to grasp our situation, and all I can do is trust the promises given by our Heavenly Father. Having "swallow[ed] up death forever" by dying for us and rising from the dead, Jesus removed the final consequence of our sins and, instead, offers comfort and reassurance of His love by wiping "away tears from all faces."[7] A brief glance into many of the Psalms reassures our wandering hearts that "His steadfast love endures forever."[8] What greater relief is there for our wearied souls? While we struggle and fail every day, our Father's care for us will never fade. Not only has He ensured our salvation, but He also cares for us as His children. No matter the length of Noah's days, we cling to these words: "He heals the brokenhearted and binds up their wounds."[9] This promise applies to us as brokenhearted parents as well as to our little child with physical heart problems. Simply knowing of our Heavenly Father's great love for His creation allows us to rest in His will when it comes to the outcome of our pregnancy.

While our Pinterest what-to-do-before-baby-arrives checklist remains undone, we have prepared for the arrival of our son in more spiritually substantial ways. Instead of painting a nursery, Christian and I have been spending more time in daily devotion and prayer. We also attend the daily prayer offices at the

---

5   1 Peter 4:12–13
6   John 19:25
7   Isaiah 25:8
8   Psalm 136:1
9   Psalm 147:3

seminary's chapel as often as we can.[10] Noah has heard God's Word on countless occasions throughout his young life, and this brings us more comfort than any completed to-do list could, for "faith comes from hearing, and hearing through the Word of Christ."[11] We join our son at the feet of our Heavenly Father each day, listening to His Word and rejoicing in the promise of the resurrection.

Trying to understand why God would allow for any of this to happen has challenged us on many levels. No medical diagnosis will ever satisfy our human hunger for understanding nor our demand for resolution to the question of life and death. The only place where we can find true answers and reassurance is in God's Word where He establishes that He does not wish for any of us to suffer and die.[12] Exactly for this reason, God sent us His own Son, Jesus, to suffer and die in our place, that "whoever believes in [Him], though he die, yet shall he live."[13]

It is through Jesus' sacrifice that God reveals His will for us. He answers all of my desperate "Why?" pleas with that one definitive and final act. Christ's death and resurrection have freed us from the power of sin, death, and the devil. While I certainly fail to rejoice in this freedom on many occasions, I am thankful that God promises eternal life to me and my son, for we both will physically die one day. I can take comfort in knowing that this present suffering is not a specific punishment for my own actions but is, in fact, simply one of the numerous effects of our sinful human condition.[14] During His earthly ministry, Jesus addressed this very matter when He healed a man born blind and taught, "It was not that this man sinned, or his parents, but that the works of God might be displayed in him."[15] This explanation for the existence of illness in the world does not make the reality of

---

10   Christian is in the midst of his seminary studies. His school holds daily services for the faculty, students, and their families.
11   Romans 10:17
12   Ezekiel 33:11
13   John 11:25; 1 John 4:9–10
14   Romans 8:18–22
15   John 9:3

Noah's troubles any less serious, and yet it does make our current and future struggles seem bearable.

Our gracious Lord has freed us from the eternal consequences of our actions, and there is the proof of His love. Suffering may still come to us, overpower us, and scatter our plans into the wind, but we can always—no matter the circumstances—look forward to the day our battles will cease when we join our Father in life everlasting.

Thanks to more time for personal devotions, I also have learned that we are not as alone in this ordeal as I thought. Reading through the trials of Job in the Old Testament, especially, has brought me immeasurable comfort, for if anyone walked "through the valley of the shadow of death,"[16] it was Job. This tortured man, upon learning that his own children had perished, faithfully confessed, "The LORD gave, and the LORD has taken away; blessed be the name of the LORD."[17] I can only hope and pray to have a similar confession on my lips—to fall to the ground in worship—after hearing the most devastating of news. God grant me such faith.

That God chose to bless two sinful individuals with the extraordinary vocation of parenthood remains the most humbling reality for us. Not only has little Noah helped us and so many others to recognize the wonderful miracle of life, he has forced us as parents to return to our Heavenly Father, who uses our greatest sorrows to guide us back to His never-ending love and care. For we may be "sure that neither death nor life, nor angels nor rulers, nor things present nor things to come, nor powers, nor height nor depth, nor anything else in all creation, will be able to separate us from the love of God in Christ Jesus our Lord."[18]

Just as God formed each and every one of us, He also formed Noah's little body exactly the way it is for one very specific reason: to give us the opportunity to love and value his life no matter the circumstances. These trials strengthen us, even if we fail to notice initially, so that we might endure and grow in our faith.

16   Psalm 23:4
17   Job 1:21
18   Romans 8:38–39

Setting aside our own comfort, Christian and I have learned how to cherish the child graciously given to us and to advocate for our son's life by seeking the best possible care for him. While we do not know whether to prepare for life or death in the next few weeks, we continue to pray for and love this new life joining our family, no matter the length of his days.

> Children of the heav'nly Father
> Safely in His bosom gather;
>   Nestling bird nor star in heaven
>   Such a refuge e'er was given.
>
> God His own doth tend and nourish;
> In His holy courts they flourish.
>   From all evil things He spares them;
>   In His mighty arms He bears them.
>
> Neither life nor death shall ever
> From the Lord His children sever;
>   Unto them His grace He showeth,
>   And their sorrows all He knoweth.
>
> Though He giveth or He taketh,
> God His children ne'er forsaketh;
>   His the loving purpose solely
>   To preserve them pure and holy.[19]

---

19 "Children of the Heavenly Father" by Carolina Sandell Berg, tr. Ernst W. Olson. © Augsburg Publishing House. Used with permission.

CHAPTER EIGHT

When God Is Hiding

by Deaconess Heidi D. Sias

"For You are with me."
Psalm 23:4

After several years of not seeing medical specialists for my mysterious symptoms, here I was, sitting in a neurologist's exam room *again*. The memories—years of tests, procedures, and doctor visits—washed over me like waves, a riptide of disappointments, threatening to knock me off my feet and drown me forever in a sea devoid of diagnosis or relief.

Thirteen years earlier, I had begun experiencing inexplicable symptoms, so naturally I went to the doctor to find out what could be done to make them better. Only this time there was no quick answer, no "magic pill" that would restore me. The first doctor prescribed a bunch of medications to try to resolve the debilitating symptoms: constant dizziness and headaches, weakness and fatigue, pain and muscle spasms. Imagine a zombie weakly trying to get ready in the morning, entangled in a boa constrictor doing its worst around the torso—not a pretty picture. This doctor put me on and took me off medications at a rapid rate, too rapid in fact—I eventually landed in the emergency room. None of the medications helped, and most made me feel worse. What was happening to me? My life seemed to be in a tailspin.

The next five or six years brought more doctors, more tests, more procedures, more medications, more terrible side effects, and even a surgery thrown in for good measure. Still I had no answers and no relief, just lots of poking and prodding. Doctors provided their own potluck of reactions as well: kindness, rudeness, attentiveness, ignorance, compassion, and skepticism—but none really knew what to do with me.

Through all of that, I felt like the woman in the great crowd following Jesus "who had suffered much under many physicians, and had spent all that she had, and was no better but rather grew worse."[1] My life seemed out of control. I felt I had nowhere to turn and no one who understood what I was experiencing. Anger welled up inside of me. I was alone and miserable, just going through the motions of life. Where was God, and why wouldn't He help me?

One night I sat in my car in a parking lot, my eyes closed and head resting on the steering wheel, trying to gather the motivation to keep going. I phoned my husband, John, and the tears started to flow.

"I feel like I can't hang on anymore," I confessed. "How long can I endure this?"

He reassured me that things would be okay, and then he said, "Even when you feel like you can't hang on anymore, God hangs on to you—and He won't let go."

I wept as I remembered these wonderful promises of God, that He will never leave me nor forsake me[2] nor allow anyone to snatch me out of His hand.[3] My weary, broken body rested gently in His hands that night, and His Word gave me strength to go on. While I felt afflicted in every way, I was not crushed; I was perplexed about what was happening, but I was not driven to despair; I felt struck down, but I was not destroyed.[4]

Our Lord was with me, and He would never let go.

------

1   Mark 5:26
2   Hebrews 13:5
3   John 10:28
4   2 Corinthians 4:8–9

A short time later a friend pointed out that it was possible doctors may never figure out what is wrong. I was taken aback—that was something I did not want to hear, and I was angry she said it. I was suffering, and I wanted answers. I wanted healing. Sometimes, though, a good friend tells you what you need to hear, rather than what you want to hear. Instead of telling me that I would get better, which she could not promise, she pointed me to Christ. Jesus does not promise answers to my suffering, but He does say, "My grace is sufficient for you, for My power is made perfect in weakness."[5] I was a physical and emotional wreck, crying out to God for mercy, but it was only through this weakness that I could understand that my only strength is Christ's. "For when I am weak, then I am strong."[6]

So, after several years of avoiding doctors and enduring symptoms, a troubling new issue and a change in my brain MRI (discovered not by a doctor but by my internist's nurse practitioner) had washed me back in to a neurologist's office, but below the surface I felt the riptide pulling me further out. When the neurologist finally entered the exam room, he greeted my husband and me with a smile. Young, personable, and confident, he listened intently to my story—my suffering—before expressing his thoughts and concerns. He ordered more dreadful tests: contrast MRIs, blood tests, shots, and a lumbar puncture—oh, the lumbar puncture.

Medical appointments came fast and furious over the next few months, an ordeal we shared with no one, for fear it would be just another dead end. The day of the dreaded lumbar puncture arrived, and John and I finally shared our burden with a trusted friend, a pastor who would care for us during this tense and uncertain time. The pastor met us at the hospital on the day of the lumbar puncture; he shared Christ's saving Gospel in a devotion and a prayer for our comfort, peace, and strength through this trial. He and John served as God's ministering hands to me in that moment as I waited to be called back by the nurse. I knew God was with me as I walked into the procedure room and lay down

---

5   2 Corinthians 12:9
6   2 Corinthians 12:10

on my side. Nonetheless, as my spinal fluid dripped slowly into a vial, the undeniable reality of what was happening and what this might mean caused tears to run slowly down my face.

For three weeks following the lumbar puncture, spinal headaches made it feel like someone had removed my brain's shock absorber at the base of my skull. Lying down was the only remedy to the pain, so I spent the entire first week on my back, trying to do work for my deaconess internship as best I could from a supine position.

Finally, the awaited appointment for test results arrived. The doctor, sincere and direct but compassionate, explained that although my condition seemed stable for the time being, I had multiple brain lesions that had increased in size and number since my original MRI thirteen years earlier. This change indicated a serious neurological condition that could be treated but had no known cure. He explained possible treatments for the symptoms, which were a result of the nerve damage, as well as treatment plans to help prevent further damage from occurring. Unfortunately, these treatments often come with significant, unpleasant side effects.

While deep down we suspected this diagnosis was coming, such a diagnosis is still difficult to hear when it actually comes. I finally had my answer, though ironically there was no comfort in it. Lots of questions and torturous unknowns remained. It would be easy to turn inward, to dwell on it and feel sorry for myself, to try to escape the suffering or be consumed with treatment options. Easy, until the mind games once again suck me into a miserable, lonely, navel-gazing despair.

It is harder for me to accept my disease as a cross the Lord gave me, to be turned back out of myself—harder, but also far happier in the end. For to accept my disease as a cross is to acknowledge that our Lord, who loved me by sending His Son to suffer and die on a cross to forgive my sins and grant me eternal life, is in control. Who better to have in control than the One who loves me more than I love myself? God may seem hidden during suffering, but He knows our afflictions in this vale of tears and has promised to always be with us.[7] He has numbered the very hairs on my head, after all,[8] so will He not also care for all other parts of my body, including my brain and my spine?

While God indeed gives us medical care to support this body, through it all I had lost sight of God's purpose for His children. Our Lord calls us to the knowledge of Christ's death on a cross that won for us salvation, so that firmly believing this we may daily take up our own crosses, deny ourselves, and follow Him.[9] We each have unique sufferings to endure with crosses individually designed for us by God Himself. He teaches us His promises so that we may know His deep love for us and be drawn to Him through such crosses, that we may share God's love with our neighbor through word and deed. In this way we are lights that shine before others so they too may know and glorify Him.[10] Despite our difficult circumstances, whatever they may be, we can joyfully serve our neighbors, responding in trust and thanksgiving to a loving God who has given us all we need to support this body and life. None of us can do everything; we do whatever our hand finds to do as He gives us strength to do it,[11] passing on the hope and peace that we have received in Christ to our neighbor.

Life is a little different for me since the diagnosis, but in many ways it is still the same. I have regular doctor visits and tests to help me deal with ongoing symptoms and to monitor the progression of the disease. I need to pace myself and build in time to rest and recover between my activities, work, and travel. Some days are tougher than others, but I press on as God gives me strength.

As I get ready each morning, I look at a curled-up piece of paper taped to my mirror that reads, "Not only that, but we rejoice in our sufferings, knowing that suffering produces endurance, and endurance produces character, and character produces hope, and hope does not put us to shame, because God's love has been

---

7   Matthew 28:20
8   Luke 12:7
9   Luke 9:23
10   Matthew 5:16
11   Ecclesiastes 9:10

poured into our hearts through the Holy Spirit who has been given to us."[12] Rejoice in suffering? This is not easy nor fun, but it is necessary. God has a plan for each of us, shaping us through our suffering to give us hope and a future.[13]

I, too, still need to be reassured regularly of God's promises, as each day I wake up not knowing what horrible symptoms will affect me or what new symptom may appear: pain, spasms, tingling, numbness, dizziness, vision issues, basic system malfunction, fatigue, weakness, memory issues. My body has betrayed me, and I am reminded of this on a daily basis. I grieve over what is lost and wonder how much of me this disease will take in the end.

The symptoms often hit me the worst at night. During the day I can distract myself to some degree, but at night I am left alone with my suffering. Sleep is replaced with questioning and complaining to God. Paul, too, complained about the thorn in his flesh,[14] and Job lamented even his birth because of his suffering.[15] I lie in bed and cry out to the Lord with David, "How long, O LORD? Will You forget me forever? How long will You hide Your face from me?"[16] "Arise, O LORD; O God, lift up Your hand; forget not the afflicted."[17] In this questioning, complaining, and anguishing, the baptized[18] do not lose hope, but find it! We may lament, but we also pray, confess Christ is Lord, and take hold of His promises.

Later in Psalm 13, David confesses by faith, "But I have trusted in Your steadfast love; my heart shall rejoice in Your salvation. I will sing to the LORD, because He has dealt bountifully with me."[19] As His children, we hold our Lord to His promises: "Hear my prayer, O LORD; let my cry come to You! Do not hide Your face from me in the day of my distress."[20] Only in faith do

---

12   Romans 5:3–5
13   Jeremiah 29:11
14   2 Corinthians 12:7
15   Job 3:3
16   Psalm 13:1
17   Psalm 10:12
18   Romans 6:3–5
19   Psalm 13:5–6
20   Psalm 102:1–2

we have the ability to confess and praise His name while also crying to Him for mercy, confident that He will hear our prayers and complaints.

Through this questioning and uncertainty, our Lord promises to comfort and care for us in our afflictions: "Blessed be the God and Father of our Lord Jesus Christ, the Father of mercies and God of all comfort, who comforts us in all our affliction, so that we may be able to comfort those who are in any affliction, with the comfort with which we ourselves are comforted by God."[21] He does not abandon us in our suffering; rather, He cares for His children through His gifts of creation—His sustenance for us during life on earth—and through people who attend to us in a variety of ways. We cannot remove another person's suffering, but we can bear one another's burdens[22] and love one another.[23] Most especially, those in the Body of Christ bring us God's grace and mercy through their love, comfort, encouragement, spiritual care, physical care, presence, fellowship, and in many other ways. My husband, mom, family, friends, pastors, and medical personnel all care for me as God gives them strength. I also care for them, as God give me strength, for even those who suffer chronic disease are called to serve their neighbor in whatever way they can.

Strangers, too, are a part of this picture, as we serve each other when opportunities arise—a man on a plane helping me hoist my bag into the overhead bin, a procedure nurse who suffers with the same condition offering words of encouragement and understanding. Even if all were to abandon us, however, the baptized still receive comfort in God's promises of forgiveness, life, and salvation, giving us confidence to say, "This is my comfort in my affliction, that Your promise gives me life."[24] God provides for His children every second of every day; of course, He won't stop doing that in our affliction, when we need Him most.

The daily struggles still become overwhelming at times as my nerves misfire and muscles spasm. I want to trust that God

---

21   2 Corinthians 1:3–4
22   Galatians 6:2
23   John 13:34
24   Psalm 119:50

is loving and caring for me, but I often fail. This battle between faith and temptation rages inside of me every day. Lord, "I believe; help my unbelief!"[25] All I can do in my weakness is cling to the hope of Christ our Victor, trusting God's promises and rebuking the lies of the devil.

As I am daily both sinner and saint, I sometimes do not receive help from others as graciously as I should. The same people that serve as God's hands of mercy to me—helping to care for my needs of mind, body, and spirit—often feel the impact of my pain and frustration. Like every sinner, I grumble, get irritable, or lash out in anger at those closest to me, however undeserving. I can only confess these sins, beg forgiveness from the offended, and also forgive them their sins against me. Sinner and saint—who will have the upper hand today? "For I do not do the good I want, but the evil I do not want is what I keep on doing."[26] The medical diagnosis for me has come, but the true diagnosis for us all remains—sinners in need of forgiveness, life, and salvation, which are given to those who believe in Christ.[27]

In these failures of my *sinful* flesh, as in the failures of my *frail* flesh, I can trust in God's promise, that He will continue to work in me daily: "So we do not lose heart. Though our outer self is wasting away, our inner self is being renewed day by day. For this light momentary affliction is preparing for us an eternal weight of glory beyond all comparison, as we look not to the things that are seen but to the things that are unseen. For the things that are seen are transient, but the things that are unseen are eternal."[28]

In truth, all our outer selves are wasting away, are they not? This life is not the ultimate goal; rather, we "press on toward the goal for the prize of the upward call of God in Christ Jesus. . . . [For] our citizenship is in heaven, and from it we await a Savior, the Lord Jesus Christ, who will transform our lowly body to be

---

25   Mark 9:24
26   Romans 7:19
27   Acts 16:31
28   2 Corinthians 4:16–18

like His glorious body."[29] God daily renews our hearts and minds to endure the pain of suffering and overcome the wiles of the devil while here on earth. Even as our outer selves waste away, we are drawn all the more to Christ and what awaits us in heaven. In this hope we can "run with endurance the race that is set before us, looking to Jesus, the founder and perfecter of our faith."[30]

We do not expect to find the *good* God in affliction and disease, do we? "Truly, You are a God who hides Himself, O God of Israel, the Savior."[31] God hides Himself in these things that seem contrary to His promises—things that drive us to ask why we must suffer. God also sent His only Son to die on a cross for our salvation—talk about contrary. It is hard to understand how His death can bring life. So while we are spent on a cross—which, in the end, we must admit we can no more deny, excuse ourselves from, or escape—there we find close at hand the Christ on His cross for us, and we are saved.[32] So yes, even our afflictions are gifts, though they often do not feel that way. All that God gives us is gift, even suffering, for "all things work together for good for those who are called according to His purpose."[33]

"The will of God is always best," we sing, trusting in His promises and finding peace in the knowledge that we do not bear our crosses alone because God is with us. He is in control, so as we struggle in our suffering we can take each day as it comes by God's grace, and still find in it the joy that is complete in Christ. While God does not promise us healing here on earth, He does promise us healing in the life to come, where "He will wipe away every tear from [our] eyes, and death shall be no more, neither shall there be mourning, nor crying, nor pain anymore, for the former things have passed away."[34] Knowing this, we can rest in the fact that "the sufferings of this present time are not worth comparing with the glory that is to be revealed to us" and nothing

---

29   Philippians 3:14, 20–21
30   Hebrews 12:1–2
31   Isaiah 45:15
32   Luke 23:42–43
33   Romans 8:28
34   Revelation 21:4

"will be able to separate us from the love of God in Christ Jesus our Lord."[35]

Lord, "I believe; help my unbelief!"

> The will of God is always best
>   And shall be done forever;
> And they who trust in Him are blest,
>   He will forsake them never.
> He helps indeed
> In time of need;
>   He chastens with forbearing.
> They who depend
> On God, their friend,
>   Shall not be left despairing.
>
> God is my comfort and my trust,
>   My hope and life abiding;
> And to His counsel, wise and just,
>   I yield, in Him confiding.
> The very hairs,
> His Word declares,
>   Upon my head He numbers.
> By night and day
> God is my stay;
>   He never sleeps nor slumbers.[36]

35   Romans 8:18, 39
36   "The Will of God Is Always Best" (stanzas 1–2) by Albrecht von Preussen, tr. *The Lutheran Hymnal*, 1941.

CHAPTER NINE

Spare the Rod

by Deaconess Kristin Wassilak

"Your rod and Your staff, they comfort me."
Psalm 23:4

Your rod and Your staff, they comfort me?

Lord, I disagree.

No, more than that, Lord, I object. I fiercely, strenuously object!

Your rod and staff are the complete opposite of comfort because, frankly, they are pounding every comfort right out of me.

Lord, have mercy!

Please, stop!

Please.

Please?

The shepherd's tools, rod and staff, serve many purposes. The rod is probably more akin to what we know as a club or a baseball bat. The staff, taller and thinner, bears resemblance to a walking stick. While the staff may not have been hooked or crooked in David's time and place, for two millennia the icons and art of the Good Shepherd prominently display Jesus with the crooked staff. These two wooden tools are well suited for protecting the sheep from wolves, each other, and looming calamity brought on by the sheep's own ignorance and stubbornness. With rod and staff, the shepherd can poke, prod, guide, sort, beat, spear, bonk, or bash. These are not comforting actions. Rather, rod and staff are implements in the shepherd's hands to inflict necessary pain.

I am thrilled whenever the Good Shepherd wields the rod on a beast threatening me; I appreciate when He employs the staff to shove away a sheep bullying me. However, I am not so enthused when my Shepherd uses rod and staff to poke, prod, or guide *me*. No comfort there.

No matter the nature of my troubles—financial strain, marital conflict, the death of our son, or now watching our daughter living each day in tremendous physical pain—my self-obsessed reactions expose a phony trust in God's ability to shepherd me. I worry, I fret, I frenzy. I do not respond as piously as Job: "The LORD gave, and the LORD has taken away; blessed be the name of the LORD."[1] I do not follow the godly Christian advice of Holocaust survivor Corrie ten Boom: "Hold everything in your hands lightly, otherwise it hurts when God pries your fingers open." She is right. It hurts.

I clench my fingers tightly around God's good gifts, clinging to them, desperate not to lose them, turning them into idols, or false gods. God mandates in the First Commandment, "You shall have no other gods."[2] Martin Luther explains it this way in his catechism: "We should fear, love, and trust in God above all things."[3]

"All things" pretty much covers everything. Money is an obvious idol. However, an idol can be a person, a relationship, a way of thinking, a point of view, or a habit. In short, I make an idol of whomever or whatever I rely upon for security more than God. It is then that the Shepherd wields rod and staff, destroying the safety I seek in my idols, so I do not wander astray, all alone, far from Him forever. Unfortunately, this is not a pretty process. It is a painful one.

Lord, that rod and staff of Yours: they dis-comfort me.

---

1   Job 1:21
2   Exodus 20:3
3   From *Luther's Small Catechism with Explanation* © 1986, 1991 Concordia Publishing House. Used with permission. www.cph.org.

I do not pretend to enjoy discomfort, despite the sense of accomplishment in giving birth to our first and last babies without medication. In the middle came Daniel, easier because I was medicated, but his birth was the most painful of all. Daniel was born still. As the physical pain of his birth ebbed, the anguish of his death intensified. This was my first professional-league suffering, the first flipping-my-world-upside-down crisis, the first which made no sense. Suddenly, I grasped how life is so very fragile. I felt utterly vulnerable and helpless.

Lord, is Daniel there with You? Are you really holding him in Your arms?

Before Daniel's funeral, a well-meaning, devout cousin attempted godly counsel. "Kristin, you can take comfort in knowing this is God's will." While I am not generally quick to anger, that day my hackles flew up, and I blurted, "Somehow I don't think it's in God's plan to kill babies." I turned on my heel and walked away. Ironically, just a few minutes later we sang the hymn my husband and I had chosen, "What God Ordains is Always Good." Our aching hearts sobbed through the stanzas:

> What God ordains is always good:
>   His loving thought attends me;
> No poison can be in the cup
>   That my physician sends me.
> My God is true;
> Each morning new
>   I trust His grace unending,
>   My life to Him commending.
>
> What God ordains is always good:
>   Though I the cup am drinking
> Which savors now of bitterness,
>   I take it without shrinking.
> For after grief
> God gives relief,
>   My heart with comfort filling
>   And all my sorrow stilling.

What God ordains is always good;
   This truth remains unshaken.
Though sorrow, need, or death be mine,
   I shall not be forsaken.
I fear no harm,
For with His arm
   He shall embrace and shield me;
   So to my God I yield me.[4]

I felt like I was singing a lie. The bitter cup reeked of poison, and I took it with much shrinking. I did not "yield me" to God in the least. My so-called Physician had sent this cup, and now I was gritting my teeth, feet planted, fists ready for the battle, daring God to prove Himself to me, firing off accusatory ammunition directly at Him:

Why didn't You keep Daniel safe until we could baptize him?

What if the doctor had induced labor when Daniel was alive? What if . . . ? What if . . . ?

Why create life only to take life? Why . . . ? Why . . . ?

Everywhere I turned in Scripture, any comfort found on the page felt hollow. I wanted God's clear rationale, and I was not getting it.

After fifteen months of fighting against God's will, I waged a final battle, ranting at Daniel's grave, bitterly eyeing the etching on his cold tombstone: the Good Shepherd holding a little lamb. Truthfully, I wanted to prevent Daniel from being that lamb. Daniel felt alive as long as I was actively grieving, as long as I was on a quest for answers. I would not have to trust in God's mercy if I could figure out His logic in taking a little baby. But nothing could change the facts: Daniel *was* that little lamb, and he had already lived all the earthly days written in God's book.[5] I collapsed right there in a heap, exhausted from my fears and my tears. That sweet-looking Shepherd had wielded His rod and

---

4   "What God Ordains is Always Good" (stanzas 3, 5, 6) by Samuel Rodigast, tr. *The Lutheran Hymnal*, 1941.

5   Psalm 139:16

staff against the idol of my own intelligence, preventing me from taking comfort in any rationale I could construct. After every idol was stripped away, there was only Jesus with my one *true* comfort: His mercy.

Throughout life in this valley of death's shadow, my idols have become easier to distinguish. I know an idol is in the making when I detect excessive worry on the inside and feverish activity on the outside. I also construct emotional walls behind which I can protect myself from more anxiety than I can handle.[6] Idolatry is found not only in outward actions like bowing down before Baal, but also in the hidden places, in hearts and minds craving sanctuary. When I turn away from God and look to myself for solutions, that is idolatry.

This idolatry runs so deep that I even idolize getting rid of my own idols, obsessing over being a worrier and making more lists to get more accomplished. But trying harder leads to more failure. "Wretched man that I am! Who will deliver me from this body of death? Thanks be to God through Jesus Christ our Lord!"[7] In the midst of my idol-making, the Shepherd brings out His rod and staff to defend me against myself. In His faithfulness, He promises that even my idolatrous scheming does not separate me from Him.[8] Hymn writer Paul Gerhardt beautifully paraphrases this promise:

> No angel and no gladness,
>   No throne, no pomp, no show,
> No love, no hate, no sadness,
>   No pain, no depth of woe,
> No scheming, no contrivance,
>   No subtle thing or great
> Shall draw me from Your guidance
>   Nor from You separate.[9]

---

6   I am not referring to anxiety disorder, depression, or other clinical diagnoses. These conditions may involve thought patterns and chemical imbalances best addressed with the help of professionals.

7   Romans 7:24–25

8   Romans 8:31–39

9   "If God Himself Be for Me" (stanza 9) by Paul Gerhardt, tr. Richard Massie.

But alas, even after learning of His abundant mercy, next came a pain and a depth of woe that threatened to draw me away from any trust I had gained in His promises.

When a huge public disaster, such as a flood, strikes a landscape, the "After" satellite images barely resemble the "Before." Our family's landscape so profoundly changed one night that I now label everything in our lives as "Before" or "After."

That night, as we now refer to it, my husband and I awoke to our daughter Hannah panicked and screaming in pain. This relentless pain has never gone away, not even for a minute, four years and counting. In one night, Hannah's normal high school life of rigorous classes, volleyball, Tae Kwon Do, theater, music camp, study abroad, boyfriend—it all got flushed down the toilet.

No, no, no! Not Your rod and staff, Lord! Not on her!

Hannah was now suffering from a perpetual splitting headache, and she was quickly declining, barely able to eat or sleep. Nate, our college son, said, "I wonder if she has the same thing I had."

He was referring to Arnold-Chiari (pronounced kee-AHR-ee) Malformation I,[10] a condition that afflicted Nate during fifth grade with profound fatigue and a relentless headache made worse by bending, coughing, or sneezing. Nate saw multitudes of specialists and endured oodles of tests, medications, and dietary changes, but we gave up, frustrated, finding no relief for his symptoms.

One day, after Nate had been suffering with 24/7 pain for over a year, he exclaimed, "Mom! I don't have a headache!" It returned two minutes later, but gradually, over months, the headaches eased and now return only occasionally in adulthood. I could not fathom going through all of that again with Hannah. Was Nate right? Could lightning strike twice? Could Hannah have Chiari, too?

Yes. On the MRI, it was clear that Hannah's lower brain, the cerebellum, had herniated downward through the bottom of her

---

10   More information may be found at the following website: The American Syringomyelia & Chiari Alliance Project at www.asap.org.

skull into the spinal column, putting pressure on the brainstem and clogging flow of cerebral spinal fluid between the brain and spine. She would need decompression surgery to remove a portion of the skull and the back of the first vertebrae to relieve the pressure.

In the weeks preceding surgery, Hannah was not eating much and sleeping only briefly every few days. She dreaded going to sleep because she awoke in even greater pain. The closer we got to surgery, the more afraid I became she would die first. Sometimes I kept vigil over her naps because she would turn grey, her breaths so shallow that I placed a wet finger under her nose to assure myself air was moving. I was holding my breath, too, and my whispered prayers became very simple:

Please, Lord! Please. Don't take her, too!

The operation went well, if brain surgery can ever be considered a good thing. I was simply grateful Hannah had lived to and through surgery. However, "recovery" would be the wrong term to apply to the weeks ahead. Hannah's pain was off the charts, and we spent countless hours camped out on bathroom floors. Simultaneous crying, screaming, and throwing up is possible, let me tell you. The Body of Christ responded with countless kindnesses; her Lutheran high school teachers, staff, and students prayed and visited; family and friends loved us and cried with us.

Nevertheless, the months went on with little improvement. The surgeon said she would be back to school in eight weeks. For many patients with Chiari decompression, that is true. Not for Hannah. I thought we just had to tough it out—it *had* to get better—but Hannah was never able to return to school. She would never go back to life "Before."

The FBI has no investigative skills to match a mama bear hunting down answers for her cub. Talk to any mom of any child with health issues. At all hours of the day and night, sometimes in between retching marathons while Hannah slept on the bathroom floor in a heap of exhaustion, I went sleuthing on the internet. I directed my escalating panic and consuming anxiety into finding answers. I watched researchers' presentations, read scholarly journals and books, attended a Chiari conference, and talked to other parents. In my frenzy of activity, I thought, "If we can just find out what's going on, then we can find the solution." While I learned much, the results of my investigation did not provide Hannah (or me) any relief.

We did learn Chiari is often accompanied by other disorders, and over the next eighteen months, various conditions afflicting Hannah were uncovered. Previously unknown big words and acronyms now roll easily off our tongues: Ehlers-Danlos Syndromes (EDS), Hypermobility, Cranial-Cervical Instability (CCI), Dysautonomia, Postural Orthostatic Tachycardia Syndrome (POTS), Sensory Processing Disorder, Post-Traumatic Stress Disorder.[11] With all of these afflictions piled on top of Chiari, how would she make it through each day, year after year?

Two of these conditions profoundly affect her daily life: Ehlers-Danlos Syndromes (EDS) and Dysautonomia. EDS is an umbrella covering many disorders of the body's connective tissues. For Hannah, the primary impact is ligament hypermobility. Hypermobility means exactly that: overly mobile. Hannah's joints feel loose because lax ligaments do not stabilize the joints as God designed. This results in pain in almost all of her joints: fingers, wrists, elbows, shoulders, jaw, vertebrae, ribs, hips, knees, and ankles. Even the junction between her head and neck is unstable. To cope, Hannah strengthens her muscles and employs a horde of braces, but they do not magically solve her issues with mobility, endurance, and pain.

The second condition, Dysautonomia, is an umbrella term for dysfunctions of the autonomic nervous system. Hannah has extreme fluctuations in adrenaline levels, blood pressure, heart rate, digestion, and body temperature. This can lead to

---

11   More information may be found at the following websites: The Ehlers-Danlos Society at www.ehlers-danlos.com; The American Syringomyelia & Chiari Alliance Project at www.asap.org; Dysautonomia International at www.dysautonomiainternational.org.

fainting, panic attacks, and extreme fatigue at unpredictable times. A combination of treatments, lifestyle management, and medications can be useful, but it is a long process to find the right methods, habits, and doses for ever-changing symptoms.

Sure, it is helpful to be able to list off labels that explain Hannah's symptoms, but with each new term, the gravity of her situation becomes clearer. As her mom, I grieve the lighthearted "Before." Life "After" seems so much more complex: managing constant pain, suiting up with six to eight braces on her various limbs and neck, grabbing a cane or sometimes a wheelchair, meticulously planning for outings, and always being on alert for the next fainting spell.

While I still ask questions, I know the futility of chasing the idol of reason and certainty in things God has not chosen to reveal. Did God *cause* my daughter's conditions? Or did God only *permit* her conditions? I hate those questions because, practically, what is the difference? Hannah has 24/7 debilitating pain. God knows about her pain, but He has not removed it. Deliberately not removing the pain looks and feels the same as God causing it. So, I hold Him responsible.

King David writes, "In peace I will both lie down and sleep; for You alone, O LORD, make me dwell in safety."[12] I love how David mentions that he will both lie down *and* sleep! When I am in full idol-making mode, I can lie down, but I can barely sleep. When I do not trust the Shepherd to keep watch over His sheep, I have to keep watch myself, worried I might miss a threat or danger.

Satan, the ultimate wolf in sheep's clothing, tempts me to believe that rod and staff are God's punishment because they cause pain. Instead, the truth is these tools are icons of the Shepherd's constant, militant, and active presence,[13] defending me against all danger, guarding and protecting me from all

---

12   Psalm 4:8
13   John 10:1–18

evil.[14] Just as God's most glorious redemptive work was hidden behind a wooden cross of suffering, God hides His deliverance from evil behind rod and staff. Such wooden tools cannot give comfort themselves, but they are icons of His most redemptive, comforting work accomplished in the valley of the shadow of death.

As the Shepherd spent years on earth walking always in the shadow of death, He journeyed perfectly *for* us as our substitute. When He drank the cup of punishment on Good Friday, He emptied the cup's poison *for* us, so no poison is left for us to drink. When the Shepherd laid down His life *for* the sheep, the blood of His perfect and complete sacrifice poured out, "Given and shed *for* you, for the forgiveness of sins."

So what does this mean in the face of my phony, feeble trust in God? How can I, a weak sheep, say, "Your rod and Your staff, they comfort me"? I cannot say it.

I cannot say it, at least not without wincing, not without tears, not this side of heaven. Instead, through King David, my Shepherd said it *for* me.

I cannot say I truly want God's will to be done, but in the Garden of Gethsemane, Jesus said *for* me, "Not My will, but Yours, be done."[15]

I cannot stop seeking a solution to suffering, but on the cross, Jesus said *for* me, "It is finished."[16]

I cannot entrust Hannah to God's keeping, but Jesus said *for* her, "Father, into Your hands I commit My spirit!"[17]

Good Friday—truly *that* night—is when everything changed, by which all of life is measured "Before" and "After." And soon, very soon, all of this suffering will be "Before," and we will dwell in the "After"—the House of the Lord—forever.

---

14   According to Dr. Martin Luther's Explanation to the First Article of the Apostles' Creed from *Luther's Small Catechism with Explanation* © 1986, 1991 Concordia Publishing House. Used with permission. www.cph.org.

15   Luke 22:42

16   John 19:30

17   Luke 23:46

Lord, here on earth Thou seemest
  At times to frown on me,
And through my tears I often
  Can scarce distinguish Thee;
But in the heavenly mansions
  Shall nothing dim my sight;
There shall I see Thy glory
  In never-changing light.[18]

---

18   "Thou Light of Gentile Nations" (stanza 6) by Johann Franck, tr. Catherine
Winkworth.

CHAPTER TEN

Living the Creed

by Mollie Hemingway

"You prepare a table before me in the presence of my enemies."
Psalm 23:5

Like many Lutherans, I confirmed my faith at the end of eighth grade. Relying on God's promise in Baptism, I made a personal public confession of faith in Christ.

I still remember proclaiming with a certain amount of completely unwarranted pride that I intended to remain true to the Triune God "even to death." When the pastor further asked, "Do you intend to continue steadfast in this confession and Church and to suffer all, even death, rather than fall away from it?" my cohorts and I loudly said, "I do, by the grace of God."[1]

I do not know how much we were really thinking through what we had just vowed, but claiming that we were willing to suffer death certainly amped up the drama of the moment. And you cannot study much of Christian history without knowing that death is not a completely unexpected outcome of following Christ. In fact, John was the only original apostle not to die a violent death. He reassures us through the words of the Lord God even as we are told to expect this possibility: "Do not fear what you are about to suffer. Behold, the devil is about to throw some

---

1 Confirmation Rite from *The Lutheran Service Book* © 2006 Concordia Publishing House. Used with permission. www.cph.org.

of you into prison, that you may be tested, and for ten days you will have tribulation. Be faithful until death, and I will give you the crown of life."[2]

Usually when we think of suffering or persecution, we think of dramatic stories from history or from abroad. St. Ignatius of Antioch was an Apostolic Father who was martyred in the beginning of the second century. He was born in Syria, was likely a student of St. John, and may have even been one of the children Christ blessed. He was the third bishop of Antioch (after St. Peter and Evodius) when he was arrested and taken to the Colosseum in Rome to be fed to lions. During his journey, he wrote letters to Christian churches of the region, encouraging love toward one another and reception of the Sacrament. He even discouraged his fellow Christians from intervening on his behalf to save his life. And so he was torn apart by lions in front of cheering crowds, his bones later gathered by his Christian brothers for burial and to await the resurrection he proclaimed.

For modern day persecution, we probably think of people suffering under radical Islam or totalitarian regimes. I had the privilege of meeting a man named Habila Adamu several years ago. He told the story of how he was at home with his wife and kids in the Yobe state of Northern Nigeria when visitors stopped by. He opened the door, shocked to find gunmen wearing robes and masks.

They demanded he step outside and they peppered him with questions. What was his name? Habila Adamu. Was he a member of the Nigerian police? No. Was he a soldier? No. Was he a member of the state security service? No. He told them he was a businessman. "Okay, are you a Christian?" they asked.

"I am a Christian," Habila said.

Initially fearful, Habila came to terms with the realization that it was the day of his death. He began praying for strength, forgiveness, and salvation.

The gunmen, who were part of the ISIS-affiliated terrorist group Boko Haram, wanted to know why he was not Muslim and

---

2   Revelation 2:10

told him they would spare his life if he renounced his faith. His wife begged him to do what he needed to do to live. But he told them he was ready to die as a Christian. Before he could even get the statement out a second time, they shot him in the face.

Everyone thought he was dead. The gunmen were shouting, "Allahu Akbar!" His wife began sobbing. Even Habila was waiting for an angel to come and take him to heaven. Somehow he survived, the sole survivor of a Boko Haram attack on all the Christian men in his village.

Habila shares his story—as he did before a Congressional subcommittee—so that he can tell people, as the apostle Paul writes in his letter to the Philippians, "For to me to live is Christ, and to die is gain."[3]

We like to imagine that if terrorists besieged our home, we would face martyrdom bravely. But how well are we handling the minor persecutions we face as Christians in the United States?

Are we sure we would face down a terrorist's gun when we cannot even be trusted to avoid watching films and television shows that mock our faith?

Are we sure we would walk pleasantly to our martyrdom when we grumble about going to church or having to do more work there than fellow congregants?

At my confirmation, my pastor (a.k.a. Dad) practiced the tradition of giving each confirmand a Bible verse for comfort in life. Mine is Romans 1:16—"For I am not ashamed of the gospel of Christ, for it is the power of God to salvation for everyone who believes, for the Jew first and also for the Greek."

It has turned out to be a perfect verse for my life in the public square, where I have spent decades as a journalist and political commentator. Though I grew up in a pastor's family, my career now is spent in the midst of many people with limited interest in Christianity or the values that Christianity upholds and promotes. My parents always taught me that what we believed was different than what many of our beloved American friends, family, and

---

3   Philippians 1:21

neighbors believed. It was good advice that enabled me to be less shocked when I encountered worldviews and perspectives that were lacking a Christ-centered focus.

My parents also encouraged me to care for the least among us. For much of my life that has meant speaking up about the gift of life and speaking against the evil of abortion. As a media critic, I have focused on the scandal of an American media regime that openly promotes the killing of unborn children. The pushback from those who support abortion on demand has been rough. One time when I was trying to shame reporters into covering a particularly gruesome story of a serial murderer abortionist, the pushback was so intense that I remember collapsing in my husband's arms at the end of the night and sobbing. I seem tougher in my writing and television appearances than I actually am.

Sometimes it is the little things that trip me up. A few years ago, I had to do a television appearance on the evening of Ash Wednesday. Our pastor generally counsels us to leave ashes on until we bathe at night, but I was self-conscious about the huge black cross my pastor had marked on my forehead with ashes. There is a funny image I saw once that illustrated the different types of crosses that pastors put on people's foreheads on Ash Wednesday. So, for example, "The Blob" is just a circular smudge. The "Load Toner" is so light you can barely see it. But I had a combination of "First in Line"—a perfectly executed cross—and "Father's Revenge"—a huge black mark that could be seen from blocks away.

Sure enough, when I went on television that night, the comments started rolling in. Dozens if not hundreds of people took to social media to ask what in the world the black mark on my forehead was. But I also received dozens of emails from people who were watching, who asked me what was going on, told me that I helped remind them to get to church, or thanked me for not chucking my faith at the door when I went to work. I even got an invitation from someone at the Vatican to come speak about public witness.

There have been many difficult days and nights. I have received a great deal of criticism when I have written in support of the sanctity of human life, in support of natural marriage, and in support of orthodox faith practices. Sometimes people attack my looks or question my fitness as a mother. Frequently, they attack my Christian faith.

I have learned a few helpful tips for coping with the avalanche of negative comments. One is not only *not* to be surprised by the attacks, but to recognize them as a blessing of a kind. As Jesus tells the apostles in His Sermon on the Mount, "Blessed are you when others revile you and persecute you and utter all kinds of evil against you falsely on my account. Rejoice and be glad, for your reward is great in heaven, for so they persecuted the prophets who were before you."[4] Contrary to some of the false theology of glory rolling around these days, the life of a Christian is not only *not* a path to easy living, but it is guaranteed to have serious hardship.[5] We may not see martyrdom or persecution, but Jesus Himself tells us to be glad at persecution for His sake. When you know you are speaking the truth and doing so in a non-belligerent way, it is easier not to worry about the negative feedback you receive.

Confidence is also key for managing life under duress in the public square. Confidence is looked down on by some in our culture, which encourages doubt as a sign of open-mindedness. Jesus Christ Himself tells us that the meek are blessed.[6] Meekness is a good trait. So is confidence—at least, confidence which puts its trust in Jesus. As Martin Luther wrote in his preface to the Book of Romans, "Faith is a living, unshakeable confidence in God's grace."[7] In a 1525 debate with Erasmus, Luther said the Christian takes pleasure in asserting God's truth: "The Holy Spirit is no Skeptic, and the things He has written in our hearts are not doubts or opinions, but assertions—surer and more certain than sense and life itself."[8]

---

4   Matthew 5:11–12
5   2 Timothy 3:12
6   Matthew 5:5
7   Martin Luther, "Preface to the Letter of St. Paul to the Romans," trans. Bro. Andrew Thornton, OSB, http://www.ccel.org/l/luther/romans/pref_romans.html (accessed June 11, 2018).
8   Martin Luther, *The Bondage of the Will*, trans. J. I. Packer and O. R. Johnston (Grand Rapids: Revell, 1957), 70.

Our confidence is certified by God, whose Word guides us and whose Son stands behind this guarantee of salvation, even to the point of death. Faith is a work of God[9] and is confident. God's promises are fulfilled not by us, but by Him.[10] Our confidence is a gift from Him.

It is not my job to convince the world of what is true, even if I have been given the vocation of a public speaker. My job is to confess the truth in love.[11] I certainly can try to use the gifts of persuasion and communication God has given me, but I am not judged eternally by how many people I convince.[12] I am free to speak the truth and move on cheerfully in faith, trusting that God's Word will accomplish everything that He intends.[13]

When living and sharing the faith get difficult, we should pray for courage, as stanza three of my wedding hymn, "To God the Holy Spirit Let Us Pray," teaches us:

> Transcendent Comfort in our ev'ry need,
> Help us neither scorn nor death to heed
>   That we may not falter nor courage fail us
>   When the foe shall taunt and assail us.
> Lord, have mercy![14]

Sharing the Good News of God's salvation of His people has been likened to one beggar telling another beggar where a stash of food has been found. God's good words are not things we apologize for, but rather share with excitement. God's Word tells us that we are rescued from sin, death, and Satan even though we do not deserve such rescue.[15] God's Word gives us hope in the hopeless situations we frequently find ourselves in. It gives us strength and comfort in a world that constantly attacks. It teaches us how to forgive others as we have been forgiven. These

---

9   John 6:29
10   Philippians 1:6
11   Ephesians 4:15
12   John 15:16
13   Isaiah 55:11
14   "To God the Holy Spirit Let Us Pray" (stanza 3) by Martin Luther, tr. *Worship Supplement*, 1969.
15   Romans 6:23

are not things to be ashamed of or downplay, but rather share with joy.

Of course, the greatest problem with public speaking as a Christian is that the person speaking is a sinner whose sins will be made for all to see. One of my many sins is that I fail to put the best construction on the actions of others, sometimes questioning their motives, and otherwise breaking the Eighth Commandment: "You shall not bear false witness against your neighbor."[16] My dad taught me and every other confirmand to explain the commandment this way via Luther's Small Catechism: "We should fear and love God so that we do not tell lies about our neighbor, betray him, slander him, or hurt his reputation, but defend him, speak well of him, and explain everything in the kindest way."[17] This is very difficult to do when speaking about politics! Of course, it is difficult for all of us to do, no matter our vocation.

> Keep me from saying words
>   That later need recalling;
> Guard me lest idle speech
>   May from my lips be falling;
> But when within my place
>   I must and ought to speak,
> Then to my words give grace
>   Lest I offend the weak.[18]

And when we fail—when we are embarrassed about our faith, hide our Christian identity, or otherwise yield to sin—we should seek forgiveness and run to the table that God has prepared for us in the presence of our enemies. Each week at my church, we come to the altar and receive the holy food of Christ's actual body and blood that is set at that table. God breaks into our world to give us life at this table. The means by which our faith is strengthened,

---

16   Exodus 20:16
17   From *Luther's Small Catechism with Explanation* © 1986, 1991 Concordia Publishing House. Used with permission. www.cph.org.
18   "O God, My Faithful God" (stanza 3) by Johann Heermann, tr. Catherine Winkworth.

by which we are empowered to forgive one another and to be grateful for what God has done for us, is at that table.

> Lord, I believe what You have said;
>   Help me when doubts assail me.
> Remember that I am but dust,
>   And let my faith not fail me.
> Your supper in this vale of tears
> Refreshes me and stills my fears
>   And is my priceless treasure.[19]

---

19   "Lord Jesus Christ, You Have Prepared" (stanza 6) by Samuel Kinner, tr. Emanuel Cronenwett.

CHAPTER ELEVEN

O Bride of Christ, Rejoice
by Heather Smith

"You anoint my head with oil."
Psalm 23:5

Dust and ashes befit my head, not the oil of gladness. Let kings be anointed, and priests and prophets—and women filled with the anticipation of love.[1] Oil is token of those set apart for a new vocation. It shines with the gleam of hope for the future, but my hope is dried up. Loneliness is my daily companion, and emptiness fills my future. Each day I awaken to mourning, so let me cast dust on my head and wallow in ashes.[2]

My lament is not the lovelorn wail of the world, which holds no higher maxim than "follow your heart." Mine is a cry that wells from the depths of truth and knowledge. I know that God Himself declared it was not good for the man to be alone.[3] I know that Adam's exultation in Eve as "bone of my bones and flesh of my flesh"[4] is no lover's hyperbole but rather an unclouded revelation of the wondrous marital union. I know that marriage is surely a blessed mystery, as St. Paul teaches—the very reflection of Christ and His Church.[5] I know, too, that marriage is a gift

1   Ruth 3:3
2   Ezekiel 27:30
3   Genesis 2:18
4   Genesis 2:23
5   Ephesians 5:32

which our heavenly Father grants in His own best time. I know these truths, and when the storms of despair assail my heart and soul, I cling to them as to a rock. I know, yet knowing does not do away with feeling.

"Why are you not married?"

When the question comes from the lips of others, I quietly state that God has not yet granted me the gift of marriage, or perhaps I laugh it off with "I wish I knew!" Within the confines of my mind, however, the question resounds with desperation. *Why* am I not married? I know this painful yearning is a result of sin spoiling the once "very good" world. Marriage was the crowning glory of God's radiant creation. I am not surprised the devil thwarts it at every chance: divorce, cohabitation, adultery, and, yes, prolonged singlehood. As the years move me toward midlife, I feel ever more keenly how "not good" it is for man—or woman—to be alone.

I understand that sin has wrecked the world, but I cannot understand why it has wrecked my life. Why am *I* not married? I listen to the unbelieving friend who gushes that, unlike all her previous deadbeat husbands, this newest man will be good to her. I look at the young women who want to do something for themselves first and meet their career goals before considering marriage. I sympathize with the married friend who finds her husband's quirks so intolerable, but I wonder how many of her own selfish habits she expects him to tolerate. I am saddened by the friends who think children would be too much of a burden for their marriage, only to turn around and see others who care so poorly for the children they have. I am utterly overwhelmed by the masses of my peers who want the benefits of marriage without any commitment, little realizing that only the security of commitment truly brings the joy they seek. I ache at all the unthinking, uninformed, uncharitable, ungodly variations of marriage that surround me.

Oh, Lord! You know that I would not treat this gift lightly. I realize its fragility and its strength, its ability to suffuse the blandness of daily life with beauty. If you gave me a husband,

I would honor him and submit to him and help him in all the work of daily life. We would found our marriage on Your Word and pray for children to raise in the true faith. We would not expect a happily-ever-after life but would rather live together in daily repentance and the hope of true eternal happiness.

Day after day I weep my Lord's promises back to Him: "You said, 'It is not good that the man should be alone,' and You made me as a helper suitable for him.[6] You promise to set the lonely in families.[7] True, You do grant the gift of chastity to some of Your servants,[8] but You also blessed mankind to be fruitful and multiply,[9] and I earnestly desire to live out this good command of procreation. You are the God who turns mourning into joy and sorrow into gladness.[10] Hear, O Lord! See my distress! 'I call upon You, for You will answer me, O God; incline Your ear to me; hear my words.'"[11]

Night after night I sob through hymns of cross and comfort in my hymnal.

> Be patient and await His leisure
>   In cheerful hope, with heart content
> To take whate'er thy Father's pleasure
>   And His discerning love hath sent,
> Nor doubt our inmost wants are known
> To Him who chose us for His own.[12]

Oh, that my heavenly Father would indeed grant me cheerful hope and heart content! I cannot understand why this loneliness is the pleasure of His discerning love, yet I tenaciously trust that

---

6   Genesis 2:18
7   Psalm 68:6
8   1 Corinthians 7:6–8
9   Genesis 1:28
10   Psalm 30:11, Jeremiah 31:13
11   Psalm 17:6
12   "If Thou but Trust in God to Guide Thee" (stanza 3) by Georg Neumark, tr. Catherine Winkworth.

He does know the inmost desire of my heart. I want to be united in heart, body, and mind with a godly man in holy matrimony.

I try to be patient, but the gift I desire is suited to youth. My great-grandmother was married at age sixteen, my grandmother at twenty-four, my mother at twenty-seven. My soul thrashes against the world's trend of marrying at older and older ages, but I am part of it nonetheless. Either I will be a statistic for postponing marriage, or I will be a statistic for living the independent, unmarried life. They used to call such women "old maids," but the enlightened modern world dubs us "successful, independent women." I think I prefer the honest bluntness of previous generations. They understood a truth that feminism loudly denies: human beings are interdependent, not independent, and implanted deep in their hearts is the desire to love and be loved, to serve and be cherished.

I hate how twisted our culture is. It feeds us poison labeled as medicine. The prescription it gave me was to take care of school first and then a job and then marriage, and I swallowed the lies because they seemed good for me. Yes, marriage was to be desired, but so were education and a vocation of service to my neighbor. I never intentionally postponed marriage, but that subtle hierarchy whispered by the world made me think it would naturally come along later. When later came, I realized I was a victim of a cruel bait-and-switch: "later" was really "too late." How could I be nearing my thirties (then in my thirties) and still be single? Where were all the single Lutheran men lining up to sweep me off my feet?

As desperation mounts, so does the desire to place blame not just on a faceless feminist society but on some real, human culprit. Some days it feels as though this must be my fault. I strive to pinpoint what is wrong with me. Have I been too tentative or seemed too cold? Surely I am not one of those picky women who finds fault with every husbandly candidate, am I? Other times, I hurl the guilt upon men. Oh, the disgust I feel at men who hesitate to commit or lead! Then, when a man does take initiative, he is inevitably a secular pagan who cannot comprehend that I would not consider marrying a non-Christian. Yes, of course, the root of the dilemma is sin, but knowing where to place the blame would help me determine what course of action to take. Ought I to go searching for a Lutheran husband? Ought I to wait patiently for a godly man to find me? What more can I do?

Test me, O God! Examine me and see if there is any fault of which I must be purged. I do not live in resentment of my peers who are granted the gift of marriage. Did I not rejoice when, in the course of one year, all three of my single roommates started dating Lutheran men and became engaged? Neither am I a feminist who subtly or brashly despises marriage. Would I not willingly leave behind my career and my home for a godly husband? I desire a pious and intelligent spouse, but I know that no man will be a perfect husband any more than I could be a perfect wife. Indeed, O Lord, I repent daily, and I pray You to strengthen my faith. If I have not followed Your ways and trusted in Your works, then show me my fault.

Out of the whirlwind of my thoughts the Lord answers[13] me with His sure Word:

> Seek the LORD while He may be found;
>   call upon Him while He is near;
> let the wicked forsake his way,
>   and the unrighteous man his thoughts;
> let him return to the LORD, that He may have
>   compassion on him,
>   and to our God, for He will abundantly pardon.
> For My thoughts are not your thoughts,
>   neither are your ways My ways, declares the LORD.
> For as the heavens are higher than the earth,
>   so are My ways higher than your ways
>   and My thoughts than your thoughts.[14]

This truth is my answer. By earthly standards I may seem to be merely a victim of hapless circumstances, but my heart is not free from self-pity or pride or worldly idolatry. Moreover, I see

---

13   Job 38:1
14   Isaiah 55:6–9

only a fraction of what God the Creator knows. I can no more comprehend the course of my own life than I can comprehend the vastness of the heavens or the breadth of the earth. Whatever action I may take in regard to my singleness, it cannot have nearly as much consequence for my life as the act of repentance. Have I daily repented of my sins? Good. Then tomorrow I should repent again.

How could I do anything else but daily throw my mingled contrition and pleas at the feet of my heavenly Father? He knows my present hopes as surely as He knows the blessings He has planned for my future. In His eternal vision, hope and fulfillment are indistinguishable. The gifts are already in His storehouse, but He gives me always what I most need now.

> God knows full well when times of gladness
> Shall be the needful thing for thee.
> When He has tried thy soul with sadness
> And from all guile has found thee free,
> He comes to thee all unaware
> And makes thee own His loving care.[15]

Sometimes the present sadness seems too much for my soul to bear, but even when the vision of my future is doubly blurred by distance and tears, I can yet perceive that its outline is shaped by God's loving care.

In those moments when the crushing cross of unwelcome singlehood threatens to overwhelm me, I hear Christ praying, "My Father, if it be possible, let this cup pass from Me,"[16] and I cry out with Him in faith, "Yet Thy will be done on earth as it is in heaven."[17] When I argue with God that surely my will must be in line with His, Jesus, my suffering Good Shepherd, teaches me truly to delight myself in the Lord, so that I may find that the desire of my heart[18] has always and only been for Him. As He

---

15   "If Thou but Trust in God to Guide Thee" (stanza 4) by Georg Neumark, tr. Catherine Winkworth.

16   Matthew 26:39

17   Matthew 6:10

18   Psalm 37:4

heals my spiritual blindness, I see that my desire for a husband is but a shadow of my longing for Christ.

Christ, my true yokemate, assures me, "Take My yoke upon you, and learn from Me, for I am gentle and lowly in heart, and you will find rest for your souls."[19] His yoke is light because He bears so much of the weight. He takes the crushing burden of my sin and its eternal punishment and lets me shoulder only the remnants of temporal pain. Christ bears His cross unto death so that I may bear my cross unto eternal life. My cross is not designed for my crucifixion, because I have already been crucified with Christ.[20] Rather, by it He conforms my will and my hopes to His will.

By bearing this cruciform yoke, I learn to walk in step with my loving Lord. As I tread this life's weary way, He teaches me the true nature of crosses. The marvelous mystery is that in the cross God both hides and reveals His glory. The cross of undesired singleness weighs my heart down with sorrow, but my solitary days are also the means by which I may more freely serve in the vocations of teacher, roommate, mentor, friend. By this very good, though painful, gift the Father teaches me to lay down my life's hopes and dreams for my neighbors. He crucifies my pride, my self-righteousness, my self-pity, my covetousness, my judgment of others, indeed every basis by which I tried to vindicate myself as blameless.

It is not wrong still to hope ardently for the gift of godly marriage. The waiting is not proof that God is displeased with my longing.

> Nor think amid the fiery trial
>   That God hath cast thee off unheard,
> That he whose hopes meet no denial
>   Must surely be of God preferred.
> Time passes and much change doth bring
> And sets a bound to ev'rything.[21]

---

19   Matthew 11:29
20   Galatians 2:20
21   "If Thou but Trust in God to Guide Thee" (stanza 5) by Georg Neumark, tr. Catherine Winkworth.

From my own time-bound perspective, I am often tempted to see only the denial of my hopes, but the eternal Creator is tender toward His temporal creatures. To keep us from despair or pride, He arranges our lives so that no estate of this life lasts forever. The vocations to which I am called right now—daughter, sister, friend, worker—are no less hallowed than that of wife and mother. As I serve my neighbors in these estates, I also learn the true nature of contentment, for true contentment is nothing less than utter trust in God as my loving Father who best knows what gifts to give me.

> Sing, pray, and keep His ways unswerving,
>   Perform thy duties faithfully,
> And trust His Word; though undeserving,
>   Thou yet shalt find it true for thee.
> God never yet forsook in need
> The soul that trusted Him indeed.[22]

There is no guarantee that the boundary to my sorrowing singleness will be the threshold of marriage. I may carry this cross until I die, but death for the Christian is in fact a most blessed boundary. My hope, properly speaking, always lies beyond the grave. To cling above all to the hope of Christian marriage—which God has not promised—is to turn the gift into an idol. Instead, let me cling tenaciously to the sure and certain hope that God has already united me with His Son as His bride, the Church.

In spite of the emotional tempests that batter me, the eternal Gospel remains engraved on my heart, for I know that my Kinsman-Redeemer lives, and on the Last Day He will come as the Bridegroom, whom I shall behold with my own eyes, and not another.[23] Clothed in the bright, pure, fine linen of His righteousness,[24] I eagerly await the true and final wedding day. On that day, Christ shall come to claim me and all believers as His radiant bride, and as I enter into that glorious, eternal wedding

---

22   "If Thou but Trust in God to Guide Thee" (stanza 7) by Georg Neumark, tr. Catherine Winkworth.

23   Job 19:23–27; Ruth 3:9–13, 4:1–14

24   Revelation 19:8

banquet, I shall finally feel in my heart and soul what I could know only by faith here on earth: God *has* anointed me with the oil of gladness beyond any earthly delight.[25] Thus, even now He bids me throw off my mourning and live in the joy of being not only His daughter but His bride, as He adorns me with "a beautiful headdress instead of ashes, the oil of gladness instead of mourning."[26] Let me then wash off my dust and ashes and gladly receive my Shepherd's anointing, for oil befits my head.

> O bride of Christ, rejoice;
> Exultant raise thy voice
>   To hail the day of glory
>   Foretold in sacred story.
>   Hosanna, praise, and glory!
> Our King, we bow before Thee.
>
> The weak and timid find
> How meek He is and kind;
>   To them He gives a treasure
>   Of bliss beyond all measure.
>   Hosanna, praise, and glory!
> Our King, we bow before Thee.[27]

---

25   Psalm 45:7
26   Isaiah 61:3
27   "O Bride of Christ, Rejoice" (stanzas 1, 4) Danish text, tr. Victor O Petersen.

CHAPTER TWELVE

Torn in Two
by Julia Habrecht

"My cup overflows."
Psalm 23:5

I prayed that God would give my husband and me the gift of a child. Months went by and then years. There were no positive pregnancy tests or adoption matches. I was angry and sad and covetous of other couples and their families. I wondered if I was being punished or tested.

Yet God had already blessed me richly and unexpectedly. In His wisdom, He had entrusted to my daily care more than one hundred students and their families in my vocation as headmaster of our parish school. Children were hearing the truth of the Gospel, growing in wisdom, and learning what it means to serve their neighbor. Faculty and staff frequented my office for consolation and advice, they joined our family for dinner and Sunday brunch, and together we rejoiced in our shared faith in Christ Jesus.

During a conversation I will never forget, after patiently listening to me complain about a series of challenges and disappointments with my work—and knowing the pain of barrenness himself—my pastor thanked me for mothering our school day in and day out. Indeed, my cup was overflowing with the goodness of the Lord. Thanks be to God for this good gift.

On an ordinary Tuesday, everything changed. I opened an email from our adoption social worker and was stunned. Did my husband and I want to know more about a baby boy born on Easter Sunday who needed a home? "Yes!" we shouted. "Yes!" Less than forty-eight hours later and after seeing him only in pictures, we named our son Isaiah.

In one moment, I became a working mother. I was both delirious with joy and overwhelmed with panic. Our amazing, life-affirming community offered heartfelt congratulations and prayers in abundance. The questions also came quickly and pulled no punches.

"What are your plans for maternity leave?"

"Who will be in charge while you're away?"

"Will you be able to find a daycare so quickly? Or will you bring him to work with you?"

The reality of the decisions to be made set in when a respected friend told me, "My husband and I assumed you would quit your job immediately if you ever became a mother." Had I already screwed up as a mother before even meeting my son? God had given me the gift I had prayed for, but I was feeling guilty and unsure about what to do. There were choices to make, but I was not prepared to make them.

The days that followed were a whirlwind. I was knee-deep in a building project at our church and school, which included a formal groundbreaking ceremony for major additions to the campus. My husband and I wanted and needed to spend time with our son who was in the hospital a few hours away, but there was no time to manage everything well. Friends and family generously gathered all we needed to bring our son home, and within days, he was baptized in the name of the Father, Son, and Holy Spirit on Cantate Sunday. Precious school children and their parents, congregation members, friends, and family stood around the baptismal font. We all sang to the Lord a new song, giving thanks for the gifts of life and salvation won for us by Jesus as He hung on the cross for the sins of the whole world. My cup, again, was overflowing with God's goodness.

During maternity leave, I tried to stay in close contact with all the happenings at school. Not only did I miss my community, I missed the work. At the same time, I loved beginning rituals of reading, singing hymns, and praying at home with my son. These moments were precious and filled me with great joy and peace. What could be a better way to spend my time than reciting Psalm 23 before bed to the child God had entrusted to my care?

Yet, anxiety began to increase. I now had two very full cups. I loved motherhood, and I also loved mothering and providing for the staff and students of our school. I knew I would be a working wife after marrying, but I was not so sure about being a working mother. Was it more God-pleasing for a mother to stay home with her child? Were pride and selfishness keeping me from giving up my work at school? Would people question my love for my son if I returned to work?

Thankfully, I never had to answer these tough questions alone. One of the countless ways God has shown love and mercy to me in times of trial is through my husband.

"I'll stay home," he confidently said. "For the good of our church and community and now our son, I want you to keep working as headmaster of the school."

The same husband who had been supporting and loving me through childless years was now taking on the role of primary caregiver for our son, while I returned to our school family. The school we had been serving for years now grew in import; it would be our son's school in a few short years, and we prayed that the teachers already committed to sharing God's truth there would now come alongside us in the education of our son. Surely this was a good and perfect gift from above,[1] right? Why, then, did I feel so torn?

The decision was made, and the tug-of-war between motherhood and headmaster began. One of my dedicated teachers noted that I must have stopped working in the evenings because she had not been receiving as many emails from me. She was right. Guilty as charged. My evenings were now filled with diaper

---

1   James 1:17

changing, feedings, and trying to sleep in between. I was tired and quickly learning that I could not attend to the very real needs of my son without sacrificing the productivity I so valued in my work life.

I relished the times when, as an infant, my son could occasionally join me at work. He would sleep and eat while I worked, and his mild temperament allowed me to be productive. The staff eagerly embraced Isaiah as a true member of their family, showering him with love and affection and happily cuddling him while I used the uninterrupted time to work. Students wanted a chance to get up close and personal to express their interest and excitement. Parents seemed to enjoy his appearances, as well, and took the opportunity to share stories and darling anecdotes from their own children's early years. These conversations also allowed for good questions about adoption.

"Are you Isaiah's mommy?" the children asked. "Where did he come from?" What an opportunity it was and is for me to talk with our church and school community about the gift of adoption! Our cups were overflowing with love from our extended family in the church. Is that not a good thing?

As Isaiah has grown and his needs and abilities have changed, these school visits are certainly livelier. They also no longer allow for the kind of focused work I need to accomplish every day to faithfully serve our school. His busy and curious body will not quietly sit while I check emails or make phone calls. His emerging and excited language cannot be silenced when I step into a classroom. Now, I hope and pray for a mere quick hello if my husband and son can swing by between their errands and adventures.

Most evenings, I arrive home in time to sit down to dinner prepared by my husband. We value and try to protect this important time for our family. I listen to the exciting tales of the day—parks visited, games played, and new words and sentences spoken. My husband asks about the work of the school, so I share tales of class nature walks, ah-ha moments for small scholars, and beautiful friendships with classmates and colleagues. We compare notes on how the children we have spent the day with have been fed and nourished with God's truth.

I delight in telling my story, but I long to be telling my husband's tale. I am witnessing the daily challenges and triumphs of my students, not those of my own son. I yearn to be one of the moms swapping stories after carpool, running after little ones still too young to attend school.

At the same time, I also love sharing the mission of our school with new families, planning for faculty professional development, and brainstorming the right mix of Law and Gospel to share with a student who has sinned. In trying to remain faithful to my work, I spend long hours on school tasks that leave me without energy to do more with my son. When I am free to be with my son, there is often, looming just ahead, a meeting on the calendar or stacks of work left undone.

Being torn in two is painful. I feel pulled between two identities, not fully belonging to either camp. I often feel lonely while in the midst of so many loving people. In my sinfulness, I grumble about being tired and overworked. I worry about the school's success and my son's progress. I am tempted toward despair, and I am ashamed to admit that I have questioned God's wisdom in giving me both of these vocations. I do not always have a posture of joy or cheerfulness when serving all the neighbors He has so lovingly given me. Even when I have the desire to do more, I often do not have the time or stamina.

The truth which comforts and sustains me is that joy is not to be found in our own doing, but in Jesus. Joy is in Jesus and His resurrection. What a gift we are given in the liturgy in singing of this true joy as we prepare to receive the Sacrament:

> Create in me a clean heart, O God,
>   and renew a right spirit within me.
> Cast me not away from Thy presence,
>   and take not Thy Holy Spirit from me.
> Restore unto me the joy of Thy salvation,
>   and uphold me with Thy free spirit.[2]

---

2   Psalm 51:10–12 KJV

When I feel the weight of these two vocations, I am grateful for reminders from my husband that he loves our family, loves our church, and is proud of me. I hear the comforting, frequent chorus from a dear sister in Christ, "There is no one way to care for your family." I receive with eagerness a huge hug and "Thank you for all you do" from my talented assistant.

God has given me so many people to love and care for me, to admonish and forgive me. In His overflowing mercy, He has provided for me a Christian spouse, parents and in-laws, siblings, godchildren, pastors, friends, and colleagues. These people rebuke me, pray for me, and confess along with me the one truth faith, that Jesus came into the world to save sinners, of whom I am the foremost.[3]

Both motherhood and working for the church were unexpected vocations given to me by God. Both are gifts, and both are challenges. Satan prowls around as a roaring lion, seeking whom he may devour, and he knows my doubts and fears. But so does Jesus. "My grace is sufficient for you," He says, "for My strength is made perfect in weakness."[4] In my struggle—in my suffering—Jesus disciplines me, revealing to me the idols I make of being a mother and headmaster while reminding me that my true identity, in Baptism, is being His.

Immanuel, meaning "God with us," is the name of our church and school. This name is a daily reminder that God is indeed with me, sustaining me through His gifts of Word and Sacrament. Sunday after Sunday, I hear the faithful proclamation of God's truth from my pastors, and I receive His body and blood for the forgiveness of sins from the overflowing cup. When the week is long and my sins weigh heavy, I run back to the altar where I again kneel, joined with the Communion of Saints, to receive peace from the Lamb of God, the Good Shepherd, who laid down His life for His sheep.[5]

When my husband and I host our family in the faith—the teachers and staff at our school—in our home for a much-loved hymn sing, a frequent request is "The King of Love My Shepherd

---

3   1 Timothy 1:15
4   2 Corinthians 12:9 NKJV
5   John 10:11

Is." Stanza five could not more beautifully illustrate this goodness of the Lord:

> Thou spreadst a table in my sight;
> Thine unction grace bestoweth;
> And, oh, what transport of delight
> From Thy pure chalice floweth![6]

I am a mother with a young son who needs full-time care. He is growing and changing every day in ways that delight and astonish me. I am also the headmaster of a school with one hundred seventy students and more than twenty staff members that need full-time attention. They, too, are growing and changing every day in ways that delight and astonish me. I do not always understand or like how God is working to conform me to His image[7] through such blessed trials, but His will be done.

I am torn in two even as my cups overflow. I am a mother of my own son, and I am a mother to many in the faith. I have been given two vocations that I love, and I struggle with guilt at not being able to serve them both perfectly. I am torn in two, but my cups overflow with the unimaginable goodness of the Lord. He gives me friends and family, a church and school community that care for me in countless ways, and—in answer to my motherly prayer—more children to love than I could have ever dreamed.

Still, I am looking forward to the day Isaiah joins me and my children in the faith at school.

> The King of love my shepherd is,
> Whose goodness faileth never;
> I nothing lack if I am His
> And He is mine forever.
>
> And so through all the length of days
> Thy goodness faileth never;
> Good Shepherd, may I sing Thy praise
> Within Thy house forever![8]

---

6   "The King of Love My Shepherd Is" (stanza 5) by Henry W. Baker.
7   Romans 8:29
8   "The King of Love My Shepherd Is" (stanzas 1, 6) by Henry W. Baker.

CHAPTER THIRTEEN

I Remember You

by Deaconess Pamela Boehle-Silva, R.N.

"Surely goodness and mercy shall follow me all the days of my life."
Psalm 23:6

She folds into me like a child and rests her head on my chest. So tiny and frail she seems now. So childlike and innocent. I hug her tightly once more and turn to climb into my car. I have my hand on the door and begin pulling it shut when I realize she is trying to get in the car with me.

"Oh, Mama," I softly say, "I have to go home now."

Her face is crestfallen, tinged with confusion. My stepfather comes across the lawn to fetch her. He distracts her and gently leads her away. My heart is breaking.

I don't remember exactly when my mama crossed the threshold from being vivacious, organized, creative, energetic, and full of life to this almost forlorn, lost woman. But I do remember this: It began with a conversation after my mother's surgery in 2006, a month before her seventy-fifth birthday. I had begun to notice some forgetfulness, a few things amiss, but nothing alarming—a forgotten name or word, misplaced keys. The normal stuff that comes with aging, or so I told myself. She was lying in the hospital bed, and I was sitting in the chair next to her. For some odd reason, I was prompted to ask, "Mama, what is your greatest fear?"

Her reply startled me. "Losing my mind."

"Seriously?" I timidly inquired, hoping she was joking.

"Seriously," she said. "I can feel things slipping away, and it scares me."

A few months after that conversation, my mother and I would embark on separate journeys. At first glance, these journeys appeared worlds apart. I was setting out on the first of many mercy trips to lands unknown, places like Sudan, Kenya, South Africa, Tanzania, Madagascar, and India. Each trip stripped me of my defenses and my previous way of looking at the world. No matter how prepared I thought I was, how rightly I thought I understood the people and places I was about to visit, I entered into landscapes so foreign to me that I simply lost my bearings. Everything was new and unpredictable—the language, the customs, the food— and I was easily overstimulated by the onslaught of strange smells, sights, and sounds. This stripping down of my confidence was paradoxical. It left me feeling vulnerable, helpless, and sometimes melancholy, but at the same time, a deep peace and unexplainable joy settled in.

My mother also was venturing out to new and uncharted territory, but instead of traveling thousands of miles to foreign countries, her travels took her to doctors, specialists, and, finally, adult day care. Dementia, that dignity-robbing disease, reached out with its hungry fingers to claw and poke holes in my mama's brain, slowly and insidiously pulling her into a landscape both barren and convoluted. No matter how she had prepared herself— by exercising, eating right, keeping her mind and body active throughout her life—she was stripped down and rendered helpless, sometimes melancholy, and often filled with fear and doubt. She crossed distant borders of neurofibrillary tangles in her journey, never to return.

My mama was no stranger to dementia. The youngest of seven children, she watched as her own mother, a brother, and a sister were all afflicted by this treacherous disease. She knew it intimately—too intimately. In fact, my mama and I, both registered nurses who daily witnessed sickness and disease, feared this dreaded affliction more than cancer or even dying. At least cancer was a disease with a diagnosis, a treatment plan, and a statistically projected outcome. But dementia? No, it came with a total loss of control, with no real treatment and no hope of a cure. And it was accompanied by a tortuously slow, steady decline into helplessness and dependence.

Watching my mama succumb to dementia is never the cross I would have chosen for myself. Yet I take comfort in knowing that just as Christ feared the cross that was laid upon His shoulders, so do we often fear the crosses that are laid upon our own shoulders.

At least a decade before my mama exhibited any symptoms, we talked about it. We were sitting in my living room one summer afternoon while my young children played outside.

"I want the hymn 'For All the Saints' played at my funeral," my mama said. "I know where I am going, and that gives me much comfort. What frightens me is the road I might have to travel to get to the end."

"What do you mean, Mama?"

"I mean getting something that completely debilitates me, and I can't take care of myself anymore. The worst way to go would be to get some awful, slow-progressing disease like the one that took your grandma," said my mama. "I don't want to become helpless and dependent."

Years later, she began to notice her own memory loss. The road that lay ahead of her was frightening, and she feared sliding into the abyss of forgetfulness. She feared losing her way and her place in this world. She feared being a burden. She voiced these fears to me early on in this tangled journey. When I would visit her, she would sidle up to me and say, "You know I'm losing my mind, don't you?"

I made promises to my mama—promises I fully intended to keep. I promised her I would take care of her, but how exactly am I to do this when I live almost two hundred miles away? I promised that I would make sure she looked nice and put together, but how does a daughter deny a mother who, in her disease, chooses layers of mismatched clothes and a misshapen pink knit hat? I promised I would never put her in a "home," but what happens if she begins to require specialized care beyond what I or my stepfather can give? I promised I would always be there for her, but does it count when she doesn't even know I am there?

Along with the broken promises came a broken heart. It lay in pieces at my feet, fractured by anger, guilt, doubt, and sorrow. What surprised me the most in my brokenness, however, was how much my grief manifested itself as fear. C. S. Lewis recounts his struggle to cope with the unexpected blend of grief and fear after the death of his wife, and his words resonated with me.[1] I was afraid of my mama's dementia, and I felt as if I were in a perpetual state of grief, always wondering what part of my mother would be lost when I next saw her.

"My God, my God, why have You forsaken me?" I would cry out on the three-hour drive home. "Why her? Why my lovely mother who has so much love and mercy to give to the world? Why not someone else who didn't take care of herself? You know, the one who smoked, ate whatever she wanted, and basically lived only for herself?" Like a three-year-old throwing a tantrum, I wanted to stomp my feet and shout, "It's not fair!" Instead, I pounded the steering wheel and wailed. And when I could no longer stand the pain, I numbed myself to the point of feeling nothing as the highway landscape changed around me unnoticed.

Every time I visited my sweet mama, I felt like I was grieving some new small death: another lost ability, something else forgotten, something else not remembered. She lost the ability to name a common flower like a rose or a daffodil. She forgot the names of her friends, then her grandchildren. She even began to lose her sense of place.

Once when she went out on a walk—a route she had walked daily for years and years—she got lost. Instead of finding her way home, she walked five miles in the wrong direction. My frantic stepfather was notified of her wrong turn by a call from a local shopkeeper. Another time, when driving to her hair salon, my mama got turned around, headed out of town, and wrecked the car. That was her last time driving. Oh, how she cried.

---

1   C. S. Lewis, *A Grief Observed*. New York: Bantam, 1961.

And then there was the wandering. She began leaving the house at all hours. On one occasion, she left the house in the middle of the night—completely dressed, purse in hand—and walked several blocks away and straight into a stranger's home. Fortunately, she had her ID in her purse, and the man whose house she was intruding chose not to shoot her with the gun he had in his hand. Instead, he kindly brought her home to my bewildered and upset stepfather.

Simple, once enjoyable, everyday tasks like cooking, sewing, and ironing became impossible. Even peeling a carrot became complicated. My mama had always been an avid reader; books now sat next to her unopened. She could still read the very simple cards I sent to her, but she lost her ability to write. When I would visit, I noticed that my stepfather had left little yellow sticky notes on the bathroom mirror to remind her that I was coming. Eventually, these reminders became useless as well.

Somewhere in that space and time, my mama failed to recall my name although she still seemed to know my face. Sometimes in our conversations she traveled back in time down the alleyways of long ago memories where I was allowed to be the passenger. Eventually, even our shared trips down memory lane disappeared. And with this, her fear disappeared as well—mostly. She became childlike, sweet.

As much as I hate to admit it, there were times I did not want to make that six-hour round trip to see my mama. A friend whose mother had recently died said, "You should be grateful your mother is still alive." I refrained from spitting out, "Yes, I am grateful, but you have no idea what this is like!" Then the guilt settled in around me and sank in my heart like a stone. How could I even think such a thing?

I began to wonder, is it possible to live in the tension of grief with a grateful heart? The truth was that each time my mama lost some ability or forgot something else, I felt as if I were losing a part of myself and my particular place in this world. Her forgetting my name left me unmoored. In my mother's forgetfulness, I was tempted to think that God, too, had forgotten me and my mama.

The prophet Isaiah writes:

> But Zion said, "The LORD has forsaken me;
>   my Lord has forgotten me.
> Can a woman forget her nursing child,
>   that she should have no compassion of the son of
>   her womb?
> Even these may forget,
>   yet I will not forget you.
> Behold, I have engraved you on the palms
>   of my hands . . ."[2]

God does not forget. He does not forget my mama. He does not forget me. He does not forget you. Words in the Hebrew language often carry more weight and depth than their English translations. Words like *remember, restore, goodness,* and *mercy* are embodied words, used to convey God's relationship with us. When God remembers us, He brings us into His love and mercy. He shows us His favor. He knows us intimately. God restores us and showers us with goodness and mercy because He *is* Goodness and Mercy. When God restores our soul, He brings us back to the wholeness of our lives. He brings us back to Himself, again and again, no matter how much we forget Him due to disease or our own sinful, rebellious nature.

Sometimes I still wander in the desert of my own grief and misery when I consider my mama's suffering. My anger and sorrow overwhelm me to the point of doubt and despair and leave me feeling lost and alone. Oddly enough, the place where I often find the most comfort is standing before the crucified Christ. The image of His wounded body hanging on the cross in complete humiliation and vulnerability gives me pause. It makes me suck in my breath and get a glimpse of the immense sacrifice required for God to show His goodness and steadfast love to me, to my mama.

"How do I endure this suffering, O God? Why have You forsaken me? Why have You forsaken my mama?" I ask. Instead of hearing an answer, I catch a glimpse of God Himself, broken

---

2   Isaiah 49:14–16

and suffering. Through my tears of lament and sorrow, my eyes are opened to see the tears of God. These companionable tears are comforting.

> He was . . . a man of sorrows,
>   and acquainted with grief;
> and as one from whom men hid their faces
>   He was despised, and we esteemed Him not.
> Surely He has borne our griefs
>   and carried our sorrows;
> yet we esteemed Him stricken,
>   smitten by God, and afflicted.
> But He was pierced for our transgressions;
>   He was crushed for our iniquities;
> upon Him was the chastisement that brought
>   us peace,
>   and with His wounds we are healed.[3]

God uses grief, even doubt, to turn our lives upside down so that we can recognize His love and mercy to us revealed in the Man of Sorrows, Jesus Christ the crucified. Jesus takes on our brokenness, bleeding our wounds and shedding our tears, all the way to the cross. This is the great paradox: Christ's suffering and death brings life to us. His suffering redeems us from our sinful brokenness, thereby restoring us fully to Himself. Instead of explaining suffering, God shares it with us. And by His wounds, truly, we are healed.

I find it interesting that the risen Christ still has His wounds.[4] He still bears the marks of suffering in His glorified body, and those marks continue to preach of His goodness and mercy to us—to my mama—today.

Strange as it may seem, even our own wounds can preach of Christ's goodness and mercy. My mama, reduced to mumblings and stumbling, receives her daily bread from God's hand directly through the hands of others—her husband, friends, family, pastor,

---

3   Isaiah 53:3–5
4   John 20:20

the adult daycare staff, even me. How can anyone miss God's faithfulness, goodness, and mercy in caring for my mama when He has given her people to love her and take care of her in her greatest need? I may grouse and I may grieve my mama's broken, demented brain, but one thing is certain: God's promise that His goodness and mercy will follow us the length of our days is a sure one. My mama is living proof of it.

> Jesus, Thy boundless love to me
>   No thought can reach, no tongue declare;
> Unite my thankful heart to Thee,
>   And reign without a rival there!
> Thine wholly, Thine alone I am;
> Be Thou alone my constant flame.
>
> O grant that nothing in my soul
>   May dwell, but Thy pure love alone;
> Oh, may Thy love possess me whole,
>   My joy, my treasure, and my crown!
> All coldness from my heart remove;
> My ev'ry act, word, thought be love.
>
> This love unwearied I pursue
>   And dauntlessly to Thee aspire.
> Oh, may Thy love my hope renew,
>   Burn in my soul like heav'nly fire!
> And day and night, be all my care
> To guard this sacred treasure there.
>
> In suff'ring be Thy love my peace,
>   In weakness be Thy love my pow'r;
> And when the storms of life shall cease,
>   O Jesus, in that final hour,
> Be Thou my rod and staff and guide,
> And draw me safely to Thy side![5]

---

5   "Jesus, Thy Boundless Love to Me" by Paul Gerhardt, tr. John B. Wesley.

CHAPTER FOURTEEN

Train Up a Child

by Cheryl Swope

"And I will dwell in the house of the LORD forever."
Psalm 23:6

Shepherd of tender youth,
Guiding in love and truth
Through devious ways;
Christ, our triumphant king,
We come Your name to sing
And here our children bring
To join Your praise.[1]

Seated in pews on Sunday mornings, women across the world share the gentle joy of raising, supporting, teaching, loving, and praying for children in church. We find gladness in hearing a child pray the Lord's Prayer. We smile or even blink back tears when a child is baptized in the name of the Father and of the Son and of the Holy Spirit.

Yes, children are squirmy and in need of correction even on Sunday mornings, but we rejoice with thanksgiving to our Lord when "we come Your name to sing, and here our children bring to join Your praise." As mothers, grandmothers, godmothers, aunts,

---

1   "Shepherd of Tender Youth" (stanza 1) attr. Clement of Alexandria, tr. Henry
     M. Dexter.

sisters, and Sunday school teachers, we know too well that children need our Shepherd's persistent "guiding in love and truth through devious ways." We want these children to remain in the faith, but there are no guarantees. Some women know this far too well.

Meet Lynn

Many would think Lynn, my soft-spoken friend from church, is unremarkable. She goes to church every Sunday. She loves her family. She says little and demands nothing other than to hear a good sermon and receive the Lord's Supper. She appears quiet and unassuming, but sometimes the quietest women are the strongest.

As a little girl, Lynn attended a private Christian school. Her mother spared no expense to make this happen not only for Lynn but also for her brothers and sisters. Lynn grew up singing hymns, learning creeds, hearing Bible stories, and knowing the voice of her Good Shepherd. Lynn's mother made sure of this.

When Lynn was only sixteen, both her mother and alcoholic father died. Lynn lived with her sisters until she graduated from high school. Then, she married young, never attended college despite the intelligence and ambition to do so, and moved to a remote area where her husband wanted to raise their two boys. From a neighbor, Lynn learned that her husband, just like her father, was drinking compulsively and behind her back.

Lynn has taught me that each woman who sits among us in the pews has a story. Sometimes that story is filled with unspeakable grief.

Two Boys

When I first met Lynn, I knew only that she had two boys in public school—one in middle school and one in high school—and that Lynn brought those two boys to church by herself every Sunday, rain or shine. What I did not know is that Lynn longed for the boys to receive a Christian education. She did not have the money or support for private school. Our pastor and his wife told Lynn she was our best Sunday School teacher and urged her to homeschool her boys. However, Lynn felt unsure about her abilities to do this and kept the boys in public school. She made certain, however, that they were baptized, attending Sunday School, catechized (taught the Christian faith), and confirmed in our small congregation. I admired Lynn for bringing her teenage boys to church every week.

One Christmas, Lynn's boys were available when our pastor asked for a re-enactment of Luke chapter 2. Robert, the smaller, leaner boy, built like his father, would be a shepherd. He dutifully donned the shepherd's garb. Ronnie, the older and more gregarious of the two boys, offered to portray the angel Gabriel.

"Have you ever sung in church?" I asked him.

With a twinkle in his eye, Ronnie answered, "Yes, every Sunday. In the pew."

I liked Ronnie.

That Christmas evening, Ronnie sang before the congregation and guests with his large, soothing baritone voice:

> From heav'n above to earth I come
> To bear good news to ev'ry home;
> Glad tidings of great joy I bring,
> Whereof I now will say and sing:
>
> To you this night is born a child
> Of Mary, chosen virgin mild;
> This little child of lowly birth
> Shall be the joy of all the earth.[2]

I wonder if there has ever been a happier mother than my friend Lynn in that moment. Clothed in white, her son proclaimed the Gospel of Jesus Christ, the Good News, to all in song. Our pastor, too, was thrilled that the angel Gabriel was played by a strong, sturdy male.

This was twenty years ago.

---

2   "From Heaven Above to Earth I Come" (stanzas 1–2) by Martin Luther, tr. Catherine Winkworth.

In hindsight, I suspect that Lynn, even in her joy, was grieving that her husband was not there to see, support, and hear their sons. For her husband's sake, for the boys' sake, and, if she admitted it, for her own sake, she longed for her husband to attend church, if only this one night. She always asked. He never came.

Lynn placed key Scripture verses, such as Romans 5:8, on the walls of her home and on her refrigerator where all could see. She played hymns with the hope that her husband would hear, remember his Baptism, and return to the faith. She prayed. Though some might say she was "doing everything right," Lynn felt far from confident in raising her boys. She had begun to fear for their safety. One night, after her husband hurled one of her sons against the wall in a drunken state, Lynn made the decision to leave. She packed her boys and went to her sister's house. Eventually she returned, and to this day, she does not know if that was a good decision.

Many times, Lynn has felt that she failed her boys, but she was also scared. How could she patiently, respectfully love an abusive husband? How could she trust God amidst such pain and strife? The third stanza of the Christmas hymn Ronnie had sung so many years ago brought her comfort.

> This is the Christ, our God Most High,
> Who hears your sad and bitter cry;
> He will Himself your Savior be
> From all your sins to set you free.[3]

Still, for the remainder of her years with the boys at home and no matter what her husband did or did not do, Lynn endeavored to "train up a child in the way he should go," clinging to the promise that "even when he is old he will not depart from it."[4] If only for herself, she continued attending church every week. For Lynn, few verses of Scripture resonate more than "I was glad when they said to me, 'Let us go to the house of the LORD!'"[5]

---

3   "From Heaven Above to Earth I Come" (stanza 3) by Martin Luther, tr. Catherine Winkworth.

4   Proverbs 22:6

5   Psalm 122:1

Lynn later confided to me that our pastor at that time had visited her home and had spoken several times to her husband about the hope found in Jesus Christ. This good pastor shepherded the boys and earned their trust. Even as Lynn's husband slipped further into alcoholism and neglect, our pastor felt compassion toward Lynn and the boys. He left hand-written notes with comforting Scripture verses for Lynn to discover in the pews whenever she cleaned the church. Lynn saved every note.

Perhaps one might say that our pastor could have done more. Perhaps he did not know the extent of the need. None of us did.

THE TWO BOYS TODAY

Part of this story ends well. Today, the boy Ronnie who sang "as an angel" is married to a loving wife and has a little boy of his own. Few things light up Lynn's face, now softened with age, more than when someone asks about her grandson. Baptized into Christ and now four years old, that baby is her joy. Lynn has very little spending money due to the habits and controlling demands of her husband, but she squirrels away enough to buy little books of Bible stories for the young boy. Lynn is grateful that seeds sown so long ago, watered by her Lord through His Word, now bear fruit for her son Ronnie and his young family.

Today, the lean, muscular boy Robert, who looks more and more like his father, moved in with an unmarried woman and her children after leaving home. Following years of Lynn's tearful prayers to her heavenly Father, the two finally married and had a child, but her son refuses to baptize any of the children. He does not attend church.

Lynn is quick to say that she loves Robert every bit as much as she does Ronnie, and it is true. She raised both boys the same, but Robert declines Lynn's invitations to attend church, even on Easter.

This year, Lynn attended the Easter service alone while her husband went "fishing at the lake" (code for drinking where she could not see him). Lynn would have gladly cooked and hosted Easter dinner for her family, but no one would have been there to eat it with her. She came to our house instead and brought us much joy in doing so. Lynn tries not to feel sorry for herself, but even I know that my family can never replace her own.

As I bear my friend's burdens, I sometimes wonder if there is any grief like that of a Christian mother whose child turns away, trusting solely in himself, rather than in the God who made and redeemed him. I also wonder if anything moves Christian women to prayer more than fearful sorrow over their loved ones! To this day Lynn prays for her husband. His health has suffered from years of prolonged drinking, and she fears for his soul. On her birthday he asks what she wants. "Only for you to go to church with me." He will not. She places verses of Holy Scripture where he will see them, and she prays. Lynn prays just as fervently for her wayward son and her unbaptized grandchildren. Lynn lives with a burden of prayer on her lips.

So too did the mother of St. Augustine, a beloved and influential Church Father. Young Augustine had wandered down a self-destructive path of immorality and unbelief. Later in his life in his *Confessions*, Augustine details his journey. Through all those years, his mother Monica prayed. With great thanksgiving Augustine glorifies God for saving his soul by the power of the Holy Spirit and the mercy of Christ. When I see my friend Lynn, I often think of Monica, mother of St. Augustine, who prayed for her son so fervently.

I also think of my own beloved grandmother who prayed for me.

MY GRANDMA

I know what it is like to fall away. In my twenties, I abandoned the faith. I could blame my anti-Christian public school indoctrination, postmodern state university coursework, "unchurched friends," a romanticized view of human nature, or any of the common culprits, but in the end, I rejected the faith I had been given. I rejected Christ the Cornerstone,[6] my Shepherd, the Savior into whom I had been baptized and confirmed. I did not merely fall away; I walked away.

---

6   Ephesians 2:18–22

My parents prayed for me—of this I am certain—but I think most of all I worried my beloved grandmother Lois. Bearing the same name as Timothy's grandmother mentioned in the Scriptures,[7] my joyful grandmother sang "Jesus Loves Me" with me when I was a little girl and played recordings of hymns in her home. I was baptized in the church she and my grandfather attended. As a little girl I stayed overnight with my grandmother whenever I could. We played house. She read to me. I was her only granddaughter, and I loved her dearly. Then I went to college and pulled away.

It broke my heart to read later in the diaries she left me that my grandmother, who lived to be 100, shed "buckets of tears" during those wayward years. As a Sunday School and Bible school teacher, my grandmother knew what was at stake for her only granddaughter, so she prayed.

> Hear us, dear Father, when we pray
> For needed help from day to day
> > That as Your children we may live,
> > Whom You baptized and so received.
>
> Lord, when we fall or go astray,
> Absolve and lift us up, we pray;
> > And through the Sacrament increase
> > Our faith till we depart in peace.[8]

Looking back, I thought I knew better than she did. Newly "enlightened" through education, I thought I had no need for a savior. I did not mind conversations with "God" in them, but I rejected Jesus Christ as my Savior from sin and wanted no discussions related to the Bible.

My grandmother never gave up on me. When I started my first special education assignment with a school district in another city, she sent me "thinking of you" cards with Psalms. She gave me small, beautiful gifts accompanied by a verse or two from

---

7   2 Timothy 1:5
8   "Lord, Help Us Ever to Retain" (stanzas 3–4) by Ludwig Helmbold, tr. Matthias Loy.

Scripture. One Easter, she gave me a silver cross necklace. She said little, but through my grandmother's persistent sharing of God's Word wrapped in love for me, my Good Shepherd was mercifully drawing me back to the fold. My grandmother later told me that she prayed for me every night before she went to bed. I believe her.

In my grandmother's last months of life, long after I had been brought back to faith by the mercies of God, she knew I was writing a book about the importance of Christian education. She did not live long enough to know that the cover would be the Gustave Doré drawing of Jesus welcoming all the little children to Himself. I smile with tears of gratitude when I think how much she would have enjoyed that cover. Today, children all over the world, especially those with special needs, have benefited from that book and the Christian curriculum that followed.[9] Sometimes, stories of adult children gone astray have joyous endings.

IN THE FOLD FOREVERMORE

Because of our fallen condition, our children, spouses, neighbors, relatives, and other loved ones come to us with no guarantee that they will come to faith or remain in the faith. We know only that Christ died for all[10] and that God our Savior "desires all people to be saved and to come to the knowledge of the truth."[11]

If we know, or fear, that we have already lost loved ones to unbelief in death, let us be moved all the more to pray for those whose time has not yet come. Perhaps someone living next door to us is a person for whom a sister, mother, or grandmother is currently praying. Let us support each other in the Church, bearing one another's burdens in the name of Christ, by faithfully proclaiming the Good News to those God puts in our paths. Let us pray for them, commending their eternal care to Jesus who Himself assures us, "I am the Good Shepherd. The Good Shepherd lays down His life for the sheep."[12]

---

9   Cheryl Swope, *Simply Classical: A Beautiful Education for Any Child*, (Louisville: Memoria Press, 2013).

10   2 Corinthians 5:15, 1 Peter 3:18

11   1 Timothy 2:4

12   John 10:11

Above all else, let us continue to "dwell in the house of the LORD forever,"[13] holding fast to the faith we have been given. Our life's work as women in the Church is to repent and believe, confess and be forgiven, speak and sing, love and serve, go and tell, rebuke and forgive, trust and pray. We are to bring our children to the font of Holy Baptism[14] and train them up in the knowledge of Christ Jesus. We will fail in these tasks, but Jesus forgives. He also, abounding in steadfast love,[15] promises to seek out the lost sheep.[16]

> O Christ, our true and only light,
> Enlighten those who sit in night;
> > Let those afar now hear Your voice
> > And in Your fold with us rejoice.
>
> Fill with the radiance of Your grace
> The souls now lost in error's maze;
> > Enlighten those whose inmost minds
> > Some dark delusion haunts and blinds.
>
> O gently call those gone astray
> That they may find the saving way!
> > Let ev'ry conscience sore oppressed
> > In You find peace and heav'nly rest.
>
> Shine on the darkened and the cold;
> Recall the wand'rers to Your fold,
> > Unite all those who walk apart;
> > Confirm the weak and doubting heart,
>
> That they with us may evermore
> Such grace with wond'ring thanks adore
> > And endless praise to You be giv'n
> > By all Your Church in earth and heav'n.[17]

---

13   Psalm 23:6
14   Luke 18:16
15   Numbers 14:18
16   Ezekiel 34:11–16
17   "O Christ, Our True and Only Light" by Johann Heermann, tr. Catherine Winkworth.

A PASTORAL RESPONSE

A Broken and Contrite Body and Soul, the Lord Does Not Despise

Rev. Dr. D. Richard Stuckwisch

It is a broken world that we live in, and every one of us is broken in a variety of ways. All men die because all men sin.[1] That goes for all the women too. We are but mortal, and all of creation has been subjected to futility as a curse and consequence of human sin.[2] Everything is perishing. Like the grass and its flower, here today and gone tomorrow, we people wither and fade back into dust.[3] It is that brokenness of sin and death that afflicts us on all sides, within and without.

And yet, we are not without consolation or hope. In the world we have many troubles, but Christ has overcome the world of sin and death. While each of us and everything around us is perishing, the Word of the Lord stands fast and endures forever. That is the Word that is preached to you. It is the Word of the cross and resurrection of Christ Jesus, in whom we live, even though we die.

The stories told in this book are poignant examples of the hurts and fears, the sins and griefs and sorrows that confront the children of Adam and Eve. They resonate because they are so painfully familiar, whether cutting close to our own homes and families or echoing the lives and losses of our friends. The truth is that many other stories could likewise be told, each one unique in itself, yet all of them sharing the common burden and curse of

---

1   Romans 5:12–14
2   Romans 8:19–21; Genesis 3:16–19
3   Genesis 3:19; Isaiah 40:6–8; 1 Peter 1:24–25

sin and death. Those enemies of God and His people too often afflict the most personal and deepest aspects of this body and life.[4]

What is most striking and significant in all of these stories, however, is their expression of such hope and confidence in the grace and mercy and providential care of the Lord. Not the saccharin and sappy optimism of greeting card sentimentality, but a profound confession of the hidden joy and glory of the cross of Christ. It is the hope and confidence of faith in the forgiveness of sins, the resurrection of the body, and the life everlasting. It is the certainty of His Word and promise, that as we suffer and die with Him, so are we raised to newness of life and glorified in Him.[5]

All of these authors are women well served and supported by their pastors and by their Christian family and friends—not patronized with shallow clichés and false assurances, but cared for with the truth of God's Word, with His Law and His Gospel, and with the cross and resurrection of Christ Jesus. Thus, by the

---

4   At ground zero, all suffering and death belong to the curse and consequence of sin. God did not create us to suffer and die, but to live in His love and at peace with Him and one another. It is sin that has brought death into the world, to all the sons of Adam and daughters of Eve. At the same time, it is quite important to understand that the particular things we suffer are very often not the consequence or punishment of any particular sins that we have done. Certainly that is very clear in the case of Job, who suffered great affliction, not on account of his sins, but on account of his righteousness and faithfulness (Job 1–2). Job's friends were wrong to suggest that he was being punished for some unrighteousness, and we should guard ourselves against such assumptions or conclusions in regard to ourselves and our neighbors. Our Lord Himself declares that the man born blind was not being punished for any sins of his own, nor suffering the consequence of his parents' sins, but was born blind that the glory of God might be revealed in him (John 9:2–3). And of course, the sufferings of Christ were in righteousness and innocence, in perfect faith and holy love, that we might be redeemed from sin and death and reconciled to God in Him. What we suffer in this body and life is sometimes a consequence of our own sins, as the Father disciplines His children in love (Hebrews 12:5–13). And we often suffer the sins of others against us. But it is also the case that we are counted worthy, as Christians, to share the sufferings of Christ, not to our shame, but to the glory of His holy name, that we might also be glorified in Him (Mark 8:34–35; Matthew 10:16–25; 1 Peter 4:12–19; Romans 5:1–11; 8:10–23). As the children of God, we do not attempt to interpret or parse out the specific causes or reasons for that which we suffer, but we entrust ourselves to Christ who loves us in the hope of His cross and resurrection.

5   Romans 8:12–18; Colossians 3:1–4; Romans 6:3–11; Philippians 3:20–21

Word of His cross, and by the cross itself, they are brought daily to repentance in the awareness and acknowledgment of their sins, yet strengthened and sustained in faith and love by the free and full forgiveness of sins. That is simply to live as the Christians they are by the grace of God. And with that, they here confess their faith in Christ and thereby serve their neighbors with the Word they have received and by their example of life under the cross.

To those who are similarly hurting and struggling with afflictions of the flesh and the assaults and accusations of the devil, it is instructive and encouraging to consider the way these women have sought out the care of their pastors, in particular. Not that pastors can fix it all and make it better, but that pastors are called to speak the Word and wisdom of the Lord against the lies of the devil and the deceptions of our sinful hearts and minds. There is a clarity and focus in that Word, which cuts through both pride and despair with the light of the revelation of the glory of God in the face of Jesus Christ, so that the light of His Gospel shines within your heart.[6] By the hearing of the Word of Christ comes faith,[7] in which you find godly contentment and peace.[8]

Though not explicitly mentioned in these brief chapters, seeking out the care and counsel of your pastor should certainly include going to him for individual Confession and Absolution, in order to be trained in the righteousness of repentance and faith in the forgiveness of sins.[9] To examine yourself according to the Word of God, to name your sins out loud for what they are, and to seek the comfort and consolation of the Gospel is to spite the devil and lay hold of Christ. What is more, your pastor is thereby able to come alongside you as a servant of the Lord Jesus Christ in order to fight for you against the devil's temptations, deceptions, and accusations. Although your pains and sorrows in this body and life continue, you are not left alone in bearing them. By the mouth of your pastor, the Lord who loves you speaks from His cross to the very heart of you.

---

6   2 Corinthians 4:6
7   Romans 10:17
8   1 Timothy 4:7–10; 6:6–7
9   John 20:19–23; Matthew 16:16–19; 18:18–20; James 5:13–16

The real strength of the women who have bravely shared their stories here is not found in denial or defensiveness, but in the courage to acknowledge their failings, faults, and weaknesses, while yet relying on the grace and mercy of God in Christ Jesus. Their hurts and sorrows are real, as are yours, but the far greater danger would be to give themselves over to anger, bitterness, or cynical despair. Instead, by the Word and Spirit of the Lord, they rise up from the depths of sorrow, sin, and death, to the joyous hope and certain promise of the resurrection. As God the Father did not spare His only Son, but gave Him up for us all, and as He has raised this same Son, Christ Jesus, from the dead and seated Him at His right hand, there are no hopeless cases or lost causes.[10]

Throughout these chapters, the authors have demonstrated a beautiful example for the Christian faith and life. They consistently rely upon and point us to the Holy Scriptures and the hymns of the Church. Those words of the Lord, confessed and prayed by His people, establish a poetry and rhythm of life which sustain the Christian in the fear and faith of God, in spite of the turbulence caused by sin and death. To live that way does not happen by accident. It comes from living and resting in the Liturgy of the Lord's House, in the preaching of His Gospel and the celebration of His Sacrament, within the fellowship of His Church, His own household and family.

It is a shame that when we are suffering various doubts and fears, hurts and sorrows, especially when struggling with depression and despair, we are tempted to isolate ourselves from others and to retreat into our own hearts and minds. We are ashamed of what others might think of us. We suppose that we must sort things out on our own. Or we simply wallow in our grief and self-pity. The fellowship of the Church is a powerful remedy to those harmful tendencies, which not only leave us in our sin but exacerbate it. There are friendships and social opportunities within the life of our congregations, to be sure, but that is not the fellowship that is most helpful and important. It is rather the fellowship of the Body of Christ in His Word and Sacraments that pulls us out of

---

10   Romans 8:11, 18–25, 31–32; Acts 2:22–33; 10:37–43; Ephesians 1:16–23

the quagmire of our own hearts and minds and breathes His Holy Spirit into our bodies and souls. It is true that we receive sympathy and support from our brothers and sisters in Christ. Even better, they confess and pray and sing the Word of the Lord, not only *with us*, but *for us* when we find ourselves unable to speak. The Church continues to pray, praise, and give thanks in the hope and promise of the resurrection, not as a denial of our hurts and fears, but as their only real remedy. And as the Church continues to sing, so do we begin to sing, as well, in the face of sin and death.

A Christian lives to and from the Liturgy of the Lord's House, in any event, no matter what the circumstances of his or her life in the world might be. But it becomes all the more essential when heart, mind, body, and soul are under heavy attack and feeling the curse and consequences of sin. It is by the grace of God in Christ, and by the paradoxical victory and glory of His cross, that the crosses you bear and carry as a Christian actually become a tremendous blessing to your faith and life. As you are crucified and put to death in body and soul by those crosses, you are turned away from yourself to the righteousness and life which are yours by faith in the resurrection of Christ Jesus. So do you also learn to live, no longer for yourself, but for Him who for your sake died and was raised.[11] The cross thereby does away with the selfishness and self-righteousness that otherwise permeate the heart and soul of Adam's daughters and sons. By the same token, the perseverance of faith under the cross, in the hope and promise of the resurrection, is a strong defense against the cavalier apathy that pervades the culture of this fallen and sinful world.

"Not by might, nor by power, but by My Spirit, says the LORD of hosts."[12] It is the Holy Spirit who kills and makes alive, who wounds in order to heal.[13] He does it by the cross, and by the Word of the cross. The Christian life is thus by faith in the Word of Christ, and not by human sight or sense.[14] Just so, in spite of all that you see and feel and experience in yourself and in the world

---

11   2 Corinthians 5:14–15
12   Zechariah 4:6
13   Deuteronomy 32:39; 1 Samuel 2:2–8; Job 5:17–18; Luke 1:51–55
14   2 Corinthians 5:6–7

around you, the power of the Lord is made perfect in weakness under the cross.[15] That is true in Christ Himself, first of all, who bore our sins in His own body on the cross, that we might be redeemed by His blood and made righteous in His resurrection from the dead.[16] So it is true in you, as well, for whom Christ died. As you are crucified, put to death, and buried with Him by your Baptism in His name, by contrition and repentance, and by the cross that you bear, so are you raised up and glorified in Him.[17] Not in spite of the cross, but precisely in the cross.

You do not have a High Priest unable to sympathize with your weaknesses, but One who has been tempted in every way that you are,[18] who has borne all your sins and griefs and sorrows in His own body to the cross, who has suffered and died in your place. He knows your frame, that you are flesh and blood, crafted from the dust and returning to the dust. He has become like you in every way, flesh and blood like you, and subject to your death, though without any sins of His own, all so that you might become like Him in body and soul. Thus does He call you to take up His cross and follow Him, through suffering and death, into His resurrection and His life.[19]

God raised this same Christ Jesus from the dead, and as your merciful and great High Priest He has entered the Holy of Holies eternal in the heavens, where He has made a place for you.[20] He is your Anchor behind the veil, and in Him your life is safely and securely hidden with God, despite all that you suffer here on earth.[21] As He serves you by the ministry of His Gospel in His Church, so does He ever live to make intercession for you before the throne of God in heaven.[22] His Spirit also helps you in your weakness, interceding for you according to the will of God in Christ.[23]

---

15   2 Corinthians 12:7–10

16   2 Corinthians 5:18–21; 8:9; 1 Peter 2:22–25; Romans 4:24–25; 10:8–9

17   Romans 6:3–5; 8:9–11; 1 Peter 4:12–14

18   Hebrews 2:14–18; 4:14–16

19   Mark 8:34–35

20   Hebrews 9:11–14, 23–28; Acts 2:22–33; 10:37–43; John 14:1–7

21   Hebrews 6:19–20; Colossians 3:1–4

22   Romans 8:34; Hebrews 7:22–26; John 17

23   Romans 8:26–27

As the Lord Himself is always praying for you, the Son to the Father in the Holy Spirit, so has He taught you and invited you to pray.[24] And the Father in heaven hears and answers your prayer for the sake of Christ, His beloved Son.[25] In all trial and tribulation, call upon the name of the Lord, and you shall be saved.[26] He may or may not remove the thorns in your flesh,[27] but either way, He remains faithful, "and He will not let you be tempted beyond your ability, but with the temptation He will also provide the way of escape, that you may be able to endure it."[28] Thus do you rejoice, not only in spite of your suffering, but even in your sufferings, "knowing that suffering produces endurance, and endurance produces character, and character produces hope," and the hope that is yours in Christ Jesus shall never be put to shame.[29]

Not that you are sufficient in yourself; not that you are always feeling it, or even believing it; and not that you manage to stand upright, walk a straight and narrow line, and keep your nose clean, but your hope remains in spite of the fact that you daily sin much and surely deserve nothing but punishment. You shall not be put to shame in the presence of your God and Father, because you are baptized into Christ Jesus. You share His cross and resurrection, His name, His Sonship, and His Holy Spirit. As He lives, never to die again, so shall you ever live in Him.

He has come in love to save you, and He has given Himself for you. Not only in the ancient past, but even now He comes in love to serve you with His Word and Holy Spirit, with His holy body and His precious blood. He invites you to recline at His Table, where He girds Himself to care for you in peace and love. He gets down on His knees to wash your dirty feet with Holy Absolution in the remembrance of your Holy Baptism. He feeds you from His own hand, and He gives you to drink from His chalice of salvation, that you might live by His forgiveness of all your sins.

---

24   Luke 11:1–13; 18:1–8; 1 Thessalonians 5:16–18; Philippians 4:4–7
25   John 15:16; 16:22–24; James 1:5–6; 5:16–18
26   Romans 10:8–13
27   2 Corinthians 12:7–10
28   1 Corinthians 10:13
29   Romans 5:3–5

By the grace and mercy of His Gospel, the sufferings and sorrows of your heart, mind, body, and soul—of your relationships and occupations in this vale of tears, in this poor life of labor—shall not be permitted to destroy your faith and life in Christ nor to separate you from the Love of God. Rather, as surely as sin is removed by the sacrifice and blood of Christ, and as surely as death and the devil are defeated by His cross and resurrection, so surely are the sufferings of this present time constrained to serve the purposes of God for repentance, faith, forgiveness, and salvation.[30]

As the cross is laid upon you within your own stations in life, remember your Baptism, pray and confess the Word of Christ, repent of your sins, and rejoice in the Gospel. Only do not suppose that any of this is a do-it-yourself program of self-improvement. Do not hide yourself away, but seek the Lord where He is found, within His House, in the Liturgy of His Word and Sacrament.

Hear and heed the voice of your Good Shepherd in the preaching and ministry of the shepherd He has given you. Confess your sins and receive the Word of Absolution from your own pastor, as from the lips of Christ Himself. Do not be afraid or ashamed. The Lord will not despise your broken and contrite heart, and neither will your pastor, who is the Lord's servant for your sake.[31]

Be where the Body of Christ, His Church, is gathered in His name and in the remembrance of His mercies. Give attention to God's Word and to the preaching of His Gospel, not only when you are up for it, but all the more so when you do not even feel like it. Allow yourself to rest in the Word and work of Christ, and in the praying and confessing of His Word by the congregation of His people. And in due season, by His Word and Spirit, He shall open your lips to pray, praise, give thanks, and glorify His holy name. As the Church has so often prayed across the ages, from generation to generation, the Lord will not cast you away from His presence, nor will He take His Spirit from you, but with His Word of mercy He will renew a good and right spirit within you.[32]

---

30   Romans 8:18–39
31   Psalm 51:17; 2 Corinthians 4:5
32   Psalm 51:10–15

See, the blood of the Lamb now marks the door of the Father's House, even as it is poured out for you from His cup of blessing, which we bless.[33] Thus are you guarded against sin and death, against all the assaults and accusations of the old evil foe, and against the deceptions of despair.

The truth is that you are a dear sheep of the Good Shepherd, a beloved and well-pleasing child of God the Father, and you have a place at His Table, both now and forever. There His bread is broken for you, that your brokenness might be healed, and that you might be made whole within the Body of Christ. Although you have felt so defeated, so miserable, and so alone, you have not been forgotten, and you shall never be forsaken.[34] As often as you fail and fall short, all your sins are fully and freely forgiven by the Gospel of Christ Jesus, who shall raise you up and exalt you at the proper time. Then shall He restore both your soul and body, better than brand new, in the glory of His righteousness and holiness, His innocence and blessedness, forever and ever.[35]

D. RICHARD STUCKWISCH is the pastor of Emmaus Lutheran Church in South Bend, Indiana, where he has served since his ordination in May 1996. He and his wife, LaRena, have been married since June 1985. They have been blessed with the birth of ten children, four of whom are now married, and they now revel in their growing number of grandchildren. Pastor Stuckwisch received his doctorate in liturgical studies from the University of Notre Dame in 2003, and he enjoys opportunities to serve and contribute to the life of the Church in the areas of worship and pastoral care.

---

33   1 Corinthians 5:7–8; 10:16–17; 11:23–26
34   Hebrews 13:5-6
35   Revelation 21:1–7; 22:1–5

Discussion Questions

Chapter 1: All We like Sheep

1. People often mistake human suffering as punishment from God for individual sins, but God punished Jesus on the cross for all sin. Read Luke 13:1–5 and John 9:1–3. What does Jesus tell us is the appropriate response to human suffering?

2. Wandering takes on many forms. What are different ways that Christ's sheep can be led astray from the path of righteousness? Read John 10:1–18, 27–30. How does the Good Shepherd keep His sheep?

3. God sometimes uses suffering to return us to the blessed fold. Read Hebrews 12:5–15. In what ways is this discipline—this being herded by pain—proof of His love for us?

4. How can something as terrible as cancer be considered a gift in the life of a Christian?

Chapter 2: Fight the Good Fight

1. Tracy is tempted to put her trust in feelings, as are all of us. Read Mark 7:20–23. Why are our feelings a poor rule and guide through life?

2. Read John 8:31–32. The truth from God's Word set Tracy free from bondage. How is Bryan a good example of how to deliver this truth? What in the Divine Service also serves to deliver this truth?

3. One psychological approach to overcoming addiction is replacing it with another addiction—a healthier, more positive habit. How is Philippians 4:8 helpful in this regard? Read 1 Corinthians 10:13. Who can we turn to in times of temptation?

4. What is it about our particular day and age that makes bearing the cross of sexual temptation so difficult? How can we help and serve our brothers and sisters who struggle against sexual temptation? Read Ephesians 6:14–17. How does our Lord equip us to fight the good fight?

Chapter 3: What Shall I Render to the LORD?

1. Read Psalm 16:11, Proverbs 10:28, Jeremiah 15:16, Habakkuk 3:18, Romans 15:13, Galatians 5:22, and James 1:2. What is joy? How is it different from happiness? Can those who struggle with depression still have joy?

2. The spirit "is willing, but the flesh is weak" (Matthew 26:41). When we struggle with depression, sometimes even our spirit grows weak. Read Psalm 34:18, Matthew 11:28–30, Romans 8:1, and Revelation 21:1–5. What promises of God strengthen our spirit during dark times?

3. Read Hebrews 10:24–25. Our sinful flesh wants to turn inward, but Christ calls us to live our life together. What texts in the liturgical life and practices of the Church help to remind us of this call?

4. What are some practical ways to support our brothers and sisters in the Church who struggle with depression?

Chapter 4: Motherhood and Mental Illness

1. Hymn stanzas often serve to narrate the struggles and joys of our Christian lives. What hymn best narrates your life?

2. We often convince ourselves that we could not possibly survive certain trials and tribulations should they befall our family. Read John 16:33, Philippians 4:13, and 2 Corinthians 12:7–10. What does God promise us in the face of such fears?

3. The social difficulties that so often accompany mental illnesses result in many people mistaking those who suffer from them as "less than" those who are well. Read

Romans 3:9–24. What is true of all of us? Read Matthew 26:26–28, Romans 10:17, and 1 Peter 3:21. What spiritual medicine does Christ offer to the sick and well alike?

4. Mental illnesses are sometimes mischaracterized as spiritual rather than physical maladies. Why is it important for those who are ill to seek the help of a medical doctor? Why is it also important for them to seek the help of a pastor?

Chapter 5: I Am Herod

1. Read Psalm 127:3. God tells us in His Word that children are a gift from Him. Abortion is an outright rejection of that gift and a willful taking of another's life. Read Exodus 20:13 and 1 John 1:5—2:3. Is there forgiveness from God for those who abort their children?

2. Satan "prowls around like a roaring lion, seeking someone to devour" (1 Peter 5:8), and he is relentless in his attack against Eden's conscience. What is her only true defense against such spiritual attacks?

3. According to Eden, how can we in the Church best care for and support those who regret their abortions?

4. What are helpful ways to protest legalized abortion in our nation? What are unhelpful ways?

Chapter 6: Getting Past Your Past

1. What does it mean to rear children in the faith? Practically, how is this achieved?

2. Regular church attendance forms the faith of more than just children. It also forms the faith of their parents. What in the life of the Church and its worship serves as a model for forming faith in the home?

3. Not every home is one that nurtures "faith, hope, and love" (1 Corinthians 13:13), and not every parent reflects the goodness and mercy of our Father in heaven. Whatever

our upbringing, are our parents to blame for our own sins? Does faithful parenting ensure faithful children?

4. Read Psalm 37. What comfort is there for those who take refuge in the Lord?

Chapter 7: Incompatible with Life

1. Names and their meanings carry special import in family traditions. Often, names "preach" what matters most to those choosing the names. What did your parents name you, and why?

2. Read Genesis 3. In our sin, all of us are sick and "incompatible with life." What is our and Noah's only true hope?

3. Children are a gift from God (Psalm 127:3), no matter the circumstances. How can we in the Church love, value, support, and care for parents and the gifts God gives them?

4. How have your greatest frustrations become your greatest blessings?

Chapter 8: When God Is Hiding

1. Can you recall a time in your life when God seemed to be hiding? Read Exodus 20:24, Galatians 3:27, Luke 22:19–20, Matthew 18:20, and Matthew 28:20. Does God ever truly leave us? Where does God promise always to be?

2. Good friends often tell us what we need to hear rather than what we want to hear. Can you recall a time in your life when a good friend told you what you needed to hear? Why did you need to hear it?

3. "The righteous shall live by faith" (Galatians 3:11), but faith in what? Read Psalm 119:50. What gives us life amidst terrible suffering?

4. We serve as masks of God to one another. Our physical presence during times of tribulation reminds the sufferer that God is with her. To what other promises of God can

our acts of love and mercy bear witness? In what specific ways can you be a mask of God to your suffering friend today?

Chapter 9: Spare the Rod

1. When the Shepherd wields rod and staff, we may fear that it is punishment for our sins. Read Psalm 103:8–14, Isaiah 53:1–6, and Romans 5:6–11. Why can we with confidence confess that there is no poison in the cup?

2. During times of struggle, certain promises from God's Word can prove too difficult or painful to confess aloud. Using this chapter's closing statements as an example, what words in Scripture, the liturgy, or the prayers and hymns of the Church do you find difficult to say or sing? When does the Body of Christ, your pastor, or your Savior speak these words on your behalf?

3. We are often tempted to expect a resolution to our suffering here on earth, but God's promises are to be with us amidst suffering (Matthew 28:20, Hebrews 13:5), not necessarily to relieve us of it. Read Psalm 46, John 14:25–27, and 2 Corinthians 12:7–10. What is important for the Christian to remember as she pursues a solution—medical cures, a change in circumstances, etc.—to her suffering? What are indications that the pursuit has become an idol?

4. Many conditions, like Hannah's, are invisible to others. How can you show the love and mercy of Christ to people who are suffering underneath a facade of "looking fine"? How also can you support their caregivers and family?

Chapter 10: Living the Creed

1. Can you convince someone to trust in the Lord? Read Romans 10:17. How do people come to faith in Jesus Christ?

2. Read 1 Peter 3:14–17. What is worse than suffering for doing good? What does the apostle Paul mean when

he writes, "For me to live is Christ, and to die is gain" (Philippians 1:21)?

3. Read Psalm 119:41–48. What gives us hope in the face of our enemies' taunting?

4. Lutheran pastors traditionally assign Bible verses to confirmands upon their public confession of the faith. What is your confirmation verse? Or if you have not been confirmed, what verse in the Bible encourages you to live the creed?

Chapter 11: O Bride of Christ, Rejoice

1. Read Psalms 6, 13, and 139. Is lamentation the practice of believers or unbelievers?

2. "Why me?" is a question Christians frequently ask in the face of tribulation. Read Matthew 5:10–12 and Hebrews 12:5–13. Why does God bring suffering upon His children?

3. "Day after day I weep my Lord's promises back to Him," the author writes. What promises of God do you include in your daily prayer list?

4. How can we help ease the burden of loneliness carried by our single brothers and sisters who yearn for the good gift of family life?

Chapter 12: Torn in Two

1. Vocations, or stations in life, are given to us by God. What vocations have you been given?

2. Read Ephesians 1:1–10 and Galatians 4:5–7. When did God adopt you into His family? How is earthly adoption a picture of God's adoption of us?

3. Parenting is never an exclusive vocation. Mothers and fathers are called to serve a myriad of neighbors, both in the home and out of it, as well as to work for the good of their family, whether for pay or not. How can we in the Church help and support parents, both in the raising

of their children and in the work of their hands done in service to their many neighbors?

4.   How is your cup overflowing?

Chapter 13: I Remember You

1.   Faith is different from feeling or knowing. It does not find its proof in the stirring of our hearts nor in the firing of neurons. Read John 15:16 and Hebrews 11. In what does faith finds its proof?

2.   Read Isaiah 49:14–16. Is our salvation dependent on our remembering God? Dementia may cause us to forget many things, but who promises always to remember us?

3.   In an effort to point out what is good in someone's life, we sometimes say, "You should be grateful that [insert our worldly expectation or comparison of God's gifts]." Why are the words "you should be grateful"—however well-meaning—not helpful to someone who is experiencing loss, pain, or grief?

4.   How can we physically and spiritually care for those suffering from dementia, and for their caretakers?

Chapter 14: Train up a Child

1.   Read Luke 8:4–15. How do our children come to and remain in the faith?

2.   Is there anything we can do or say to guarantee our children will remain in the Church?

3.   "Lynn lives with a burden of prayer on her lips," the author writes. Why is prayer always a faithful response to suffering?

4.   Grandma Lois prayed for her granddaughter and mailed her Scripture verses during her wandering. What are ways we can reach out to the lost sheep in our lives who have gone astray from Christ and His Church? What can we do and say to give a reason for the hope we have within us (1 Peter 3:15)?

About the Authors

PAMELA BOEHLE-SILVA has the joy of being able to blend the profession of nursing with the vocation of deaconess. After graduating with a master's degree in deaconess studies from Concordia Theological Seminary in 2011, she now serves as deaconess at Holy Cross Lutheran Church in Rocklin, California. She has also been a registered nurse for the past thirty-four years with a wide range of nursing experience including neonatal intensive care, pediatric oncology, public health, home health, and hospice nursing. In 1996 she completed the parish nurse distance learning program through The Lutheran Church—Missouri Synod and was then installed as parish nurse in her congregation.

Pamela has traveled to Kenya, Sudan, South Africa, Tanzania, Madagascar, and India, working alongside deaconesses and pastors to promote Christ's mercy of body and soul. She has been to Kenya nine times and continues to provide mercy work for the Kenyan people. In fact, it was her encounters with the Kenyan deaconesses that steered her into her own vocation. She has also walked the Camino de Santiago, a five hundred-mile trek through Spain, with her husband—twice!

A California girl, Pamela is married to Dennis, a first-grade teacher, and they have two grown children, Kali and Christian. She loves a good IPA and chocolate, cuddling up next her husband on the couch to watch a good BBC mystery, reading, writing, traveling, gardening, cooking, yoga, walking, and adding to her crucifix collection. Her laugh is as big and wide and loud as her dear mama's. Pamela is equally as comfortable with a dying patient in a mud hut in Africa as she is with a newborn in a posh hospital. She prefers jeans, T-shirts, and flip-flops, but will don a pair of high heels if necessary.

When **JULIA HABRECHT** was a child attending her Lutheran school, she never imagined she would become the headmaster of a classical Lutheran school. Nor did she imagine she would one day marry one of her classmates. The daughter of a Lutheran pastor and lifelong educator, Julia was given a childhood that emphasized her Lutheran heritage, music, and the gift of words, especially those freely offering forgiveness. Her childhood home is still a place where the music of J. S. Bach is heard, theological conversations are enjoyed, and children of all ages are nurtured.

While earning a bachelor's degree in art history from the University of Toledo, Julia caught the travel bug. Trips to Italy, Greece, Austria, England, and Egypt were formative in developing her wonder and appreciation for beauty in art and architecture. This passion led to a twelve-year career working at the Toledo Museum of Art.

After years of diverse experiences and living across the globe from one another, Julia and elementary school classmate Matthew reconnected during the Christmas season. They were married in 2010 at the same altar where they had been confirmed in the Christian faith together. Julia then moved across the country to Alexandria, Virginia, where she quickly began work in their parish school at Immanuel Lutheran Church. God blessed Julia and Matthew with a son, Isaiah, in 2016.

When not in her school office, Julia spends her time reading books to Isaiah, playing the piano, asking Matthew to catch her up on current events, hosting her Immanuel family for good food and hymn sings, and visiting godchildren between Idaho and Ohio.

MOLLIE HEMINGWAY was once kicked off the altar guild. Her spirit was willing, but her ironing skills were weak. She regained a spot on the altar guild about fifteen years later, after her skills improved. She loves her Lutheran congregation in Alexandria, Virginia, where her husband, Mark, and their children were baptized into the Christian faith. The Hemingway children thrive at the church's classical Lutheran school.

Mollie is the daughter of a Lutheran pastor and longtime educator. She grew up in Wyoming, California, and Colorado.

Her siblings play the piano much better than she does, even though they all took lessons for the same amount of time. She studied economics at the University of Colorado in Denver, thinking she would become an academic. Instead, she became a journalist. She has worked for a variety of publications, and her work has appeared in *The Wall Street Journal*, *USA Today*, *Los Angeles Times*, *The Guardian*, *The Washington Post*, *CNN*, *National Review*, *GetReligion*, *Ricochet*, *Christianity Today*, *Federal Times*, *Radio & Records*, and many other publications. Mollie has been a contributor to Fox News since 2017, where she regularly appears on the *Special Report* All-Star Panel and *MediaBuzz*.

Mollie was a 2004 recipient of a Phillips Foundation Journalism Fellowship and a 2014 recipient of the Claremont Institute's Lincoln Fellowship. She and Mark were the Eugene C. Pulliam Visiting Fellows at Hillsdale College in 2016, and she serves on the board of the News Literacy Project and The Fund for American Studies' Institute on Political Journalism. In 2017 Mollie received Avail NYC's Voice for Change award, and in 2015 she was named Media Research Center's first Noel Sheppard Media Blogger of the Year award.

CHERYL MAGNESS is a Texas girl who does not like heat but loves the change of seasons, so it is probably good she has lived in the Midwest most of her adult life. Some of her favorite things are French roast coffee, dark chocolate with coconut, and any cocktail mixed by her husband. As a music major in college, she took literature classes for stress relief. Now that she writes for a living, she plays piano for stress relief.

Cheryl has bachelor's degrees in piano performance and secondary education from the University of North Texas and a master's degree in English from the University of Houston. She began her professional career teaching high school, then college English, after which she spent many years as a freelance musician, writer, and editor while homeschooling her children. Her work has been published by *The Federalist*, *Touchstone*, *American Thinker*, and *The Lutheran Witness*, among others. She is currently employed full time as a writer and editor for The Lutheran Church—Missouri Synod.

Cheryl and her husband, Phillip, a Lutheran cantor, have three children: Trevor, Caitlin, and Evan. Her idea of the perfect day is one that begins in church and ends on the patio—come to think of it, most Sundays!

REBECCA MAYES began her adult life with plans to be a high school educator and to start a family with husband Ben. Twenty years later, she has spent far more time learning than educating and more time letting go than taking control.

Rebecca followed her husband across the globe as he pursued various theology degrees. Along the way she learned some German, worked for a developmental disabilities organization, and nervously scrapbooked an album for an adoption agency. In 2004 Rebecca and Ben began their parental education under the tutelage of seven-month-old Caleb, who came to them from a foster family. Ben soon finished his studies and moved the family to Saint Louis, Missouri, where he became an editor and Rebecca made the acquaintance of Katie Schuermann, fellow blogger at HeRemembverstheBarren.com. Rebecca also had the opportunity to study cultural differences up close at her family's inner-city congregation, organizing volunteer groups to provide childcare for the diverse clients of a crisis pregnancy center. In 2012 the Lord gifted her and Ben with a second son, Jonathan, delivered to them on Memorial Day, not by a doctor in a delivery room, but by a social worker in a parking lot.

In 2016 Ben was called to be a professor at Concordia Theological Seminary in Fort Wayne, Indiana. The family now lives on campus where Rebecca has the pleasure of hosting guests and assisting with the care network for faculty and staff families. Rebecca and Ben homeschool both sons, and Rebecca now spends one day a week being the "lead learner" of a group of homeschool teenagers as they use a classical approach to understand and analyze the world around them.

These days Rebecca finds her greatest joys in waking up every morning next to a handsome theologian, listening to Jonathan beginning to read, and discussing literature and history with Caleb. Her favorite days are when she and her three guys are exploring the great outdoors together and dreaming about how to get the whole family over to Europe for a cultural adventure.

CHRISTINA JOY ROBERTS uses her middle name whenever possible as a reminder of what is hers in Christ even when she does not feel it. Christina is kantor of Our Savior Lutheran Church and School in Grand Rapids, Michigan, a congregation rich in unique artwork, poignant preaching, and superbly-catechized members.

Educated in a one-room country school and reared on a pig farm in Nebraska, Christina received new birth in the waters of Holy Baptism and heard Christ's Word every Sunday of her youth thanks to the blessed gift of faithful parents. She and her husband, Jerry, strive to provide these same gifts for their five children: Simeon, Thomas, Abraham, and twins Cecilia and Peter.

Throughout undergraduate work at the University of North Texas, where the College of Music alone had as many people as her hometown, Christina helped out by accompanying the choirs and playing organ at Messiah Lutheran Church in Keller. At the death of the congregation's music director, Christina took over the position. Organ workshops and the Good Shepherd Institute at Concordia Theological Seminary ignited her love of liturgy, hymnody, and theology and connected her with her current congregation in Michigan.

In 2001 Christina made the solo move to Grand Rapids, and within the year met and married her husband, the 7th/8th grade teacher at Our Savior Lutheran School. In 2007 she began the Master of Church Music program at Concordia University Chicago. Eight years and three children later, she completed the degree, prompting the kind people at Our Savior to change her job title from Director of Music to Kantor.

Christina carves out time to obsess over several hobbies, ranging from reading, knitting, and bullet journaling to running, cycling, and orienteering.

KATIE SCHUERMANN was raised in the middle of a cornfield (sometimes beanfield) in rural Illinois. As a result, she adores open windows, late afternoon sunshine, incoming storms, shade trees, country walks, lilac bushes, barn kittens, summer gardens, family cookouts, and green grass under her bare feet.

The youngest daughter of Bob and Cindy Roley, Katie learned to side the outside of a house from her father, clean the inside of a house from her mother, and fill a house with music and laughter from her sisters. She studied vocal pedagogy at Greenville University before earning master's degrees in both choral conducting and music history from the University of Missouri, Kansas City—Conservatory of Music. After teaching at various colleges and universities across the Midwest, she retired from grading papers and settled in Illinois with her husband of sixteen years, the dashing Rev. Michael P. Schuermann, and a fuzzy bunny named Boo Radley.

Katie daily applies herself to the art of being a worthy Mrs. to her Mr. as well as brewing the perfect batch of kombucha. When time permits, she indulges in a bit of singing and writing. Her nonfiction books, *He Remembers the Barren* (LL, 2011; 2nd ed., EP, 2017) and *Pew Sisters* (CPH, 2013), address the topics of suffering and the theology of the cross for the benefit of her sisters in Christ. Her acclaimed Anthems of Zion fiction series, *House of Living Stones* (CPH, 2014), *The Choir Immortal* (CPH, 2015), and *The Harvest Raise* (CPH, 2017), tells the story of Emily Duke, a choir director from the big city who moves to a small town in Illinois to direct the local church choir. Contrary to popular opinion, the series is not autobiographical. Emily does not know how to side a house.

Born and raised in the beautiful state of Michigan, **MAGDALENA SCHULTZ** grew up on a small farm and still maintains a deep affection for quiet, rural life. Following her graduation from Hillsdale College, she applied her studies in history and German to an internship in sleepy Wittenberg, Germany. Her experiences there led to her employment as a virtual assistant to the managing director of the International Lutheran Society of Wittenberg, which resides in the historic Old Latin School.

As a virtual assistant, Magdalena has been able to work from home while her husband, Christian, pursues his Master of Divinity at Concordia Theological Seminary in Fort Wayne, Indiana. In May 2018 she and Christian rejoiced in the birth of their son Noah and have welcomed him and all of his ongoing specialized care with thankful hearts.

When not otherwise occupied, Magdalena spends as much time as possible outside, reading, or searching for another favorite coffee shop. This is her first venture into the world of writing outside of her comfort zone of history papers and business emails.

HEIDI D. SIAS is a deaconess, writer, editor, photographer, sports enthusiast, daughter, wife, and child of God. Time at Concordia Theological Seminary garnered Heidi a Master of Arts degree in Religion, a deeper faith, and a renewed desire to share the joy to be found in God's promises.

A Chicago native, Heidi fell in love with Montana while her husband, John, served there as pastor for seven years. Under the big sky, Heidi found room to cultivate her writing and editing skills, to sow God's promises at pastors' wives and LWML retreats, and to pioneer *Lessons for Lambs*, a children's bulletin following the one-year lectionary. During her final year in the wide-open spaces, Heidi completed a remote deaconess internship with Lutheran Friends of the Deaf (LFD) in Mill Neck, New York, through Concordia University Chicago. Heidi is now blessed to continue serving remotely as a part-time called deaconess with LFD, working on a translation of the liturgy into sign language with a Deaf translation team as well as teaching church interpreting.

God's plan took another predictably unexpected turn with a move from Montana to Missouri in 2016, following John's election to serve as secretary of The Lutheran Church—Missouri Synod. Heidi's friends would say that you can take the girl out of Montana and Chicago, but you cannot take Montana or diehard Chicago sports fanaticism out of the girl! Heidi also enjoys hiking, camping, photographing scenery (especially mountains), rounding up Bailey cattle in Montana, and playing fantasy baseball in a league of like-minded Lutherans where she can reminisce about her softball glory days.

HEATHER SMITH had an eclectic religious upbringing that included stints in various Lutheran, Methodist, Pentecostal, Mennonite, and Southern Baptist churches before coming to rest in The Lutheran Church—Missouri Synod. Those childhood wanderings through the desert of decision theology and social gospel doubtless have a lot to do with why she now so tenaciously embraces the comforting theology of the cross.

Heather studied elementary education with specializations in music and English at Concordia University, Ann Arbor, Michigan, before accepting a teaching call to a state she had never even visited: Wyoming. In her total of twelve years there as Miss Judd the teacher, she enjoyed delving into classical education, baking for hungry middle schoolers, and writing humorous historical school plays. She also spent two years in the Washington, D.C., area working on a master's degree in English, during which time she fatefully made the acquaintance of a most persistent Lutheran matchmaker.

Through the machinations of matchmaker Mollie Hemingway and the grace of God she received the joyous gift of marriage in June 2017. She now enjoys her days as wife to Rev. Sean Smith, continually thanking God for the blessings He has sent, as well as those He graciously withholds in His divine wisdom.

CHERYL SWOPE, M.Ed., is the author of *Simply Classical: A Beautiful Education for Any Child* (2013), creator of the Simply Classical Curriculum for Special Needs, and editor of the *Simply Classical Journal*, all from Memoria Press.

With a master's degree in education, Cheryl has served in public and private schools and holds lifetime K–12 state teaching certifications in learning disabilities and behavior disorders. She has spoken at her state's Council for Exceptional Children conference, at Hillsdale Academy, and at homeschooling conventions all over the country. She speaks regularly at the Memoria Press Sodalitas summer conference in Louisville and also at summer conferences for the Consortium for Classical Lutheran Education, where she serves as permanent board member and editor of the *Classical Lutheran Education Journal*. Cheryl's articles have appeared in *The Classical Teacher*, publications for the CiRCE Institute, and the *Classical Lutheran Education Journal*. She also co-authored *Curriculum Resource Guide for Classical Lutheran Education* (CCLE, 2015) and *Eternal Treasures: Teaching Your Child at Home* (LCMS, 2015).

More than twenty years ago, Cheryl and her husband adopted fair-haired twins, a boy and a girl. They homeschooled the children from infancy through high school in Missouri, where they all live together today. Both children have autism, learning disabilities, and schizophrenia. Their full story is told in the book *Simply Classical*. Now young adults, Michael and Michelle's enduring love of Latin, liturgy, hymnody, history, astronomy, and literature—and their God-given desire to forgive and be forgiven—has inspired Cheryl to share the hopeful message that a classical Christian education offers benefits to any child.

KRISTIN WASSILAK is a child of God, a wife of Rob for thirty years, and a mother of three children in heaven in addition to a daughter, son, and his wife here on earth. Born at the old Norwegian Lutheran Deaconess Hospital, Kristin is a proud Chicagoan who was apparently destined to be a deaconess. She received a Bachelor of Arts in Theology with Deaconess Certification from Concordia College, River Forest, Illinois, and has served as a deaconess in The Lutheran Church—Missouri Synod (LCMS) for thirty-two years.

Kristin learned to navigate the trenches of deaconess service from the saints in three congregations, hospital staff, and patients. She particularly cherishes opportunities to speak the Gospel at the bedside of the dying and to women burdened by domestic abuse.

She served on the LCMS President's Commission on Women, the Domestic Violence and Child Abuse Task Force, and as a Synodical reconciler. She also served on the board of directors for Word of Hope, a post-abortion healing ministry of Lutherans For Life.

Her longest service has been to Concordia University Chicago (CUC) as Deaconess Director of the LCMS's only undergraduate deaconess program as well as CUC's certification and graduate deaconess programs. Treasured students, theology faculty, and staff have taught Kristin much more than she could ever teach them. Her motto echoes the words of deaconess pioneer Rev. Wilhelm Loehe: "My reward is that I am permitted to serve."

Kristin's favorite things include laughter and story-telling at the family dinner table, walking dates with Rob along the Chicago River and lakefront, fish tacos, strawberry rhubarb pie with ice cream, sunsets over any body of water, dogs, biking, camping, cedar forests, and sunrise kayaking at the family cabin in Wisconsin.

About the Artist

For the cover of *He Restores My Soul*, Katie Schuermann and Emmanuel Press commissioned an original work of art from REBECCA SHEWMAKER. She holds a Bachelor of Arts in Art History and Visual Arts from Rice University (2006) and a Master of Fine Arts in Painting and Intermedia from Texas Women's University (2018), where she also taught Art Appreciation, Watercolor, and Basic Drawing. Rebecca's work was recently included in the Good Shepherd Institute's Sola Faith-Grace-Scripture exhibition at Concordia Theological Seminary. Selections from her body of work have been shown in several galleries in the Dallas-Fort Worth area, where she lives with her husband, Tim, who is the music director at Our Redeemer Lutheran Church in Dallas. When not making art, Rebecca enjoys singing in the church choir, knitting, listening to audiobooks, and entertaining her two cats.

Rebecca based the landscape of "He Restores My Soul" on her memories of pastures near her childhood home: wide open fields bordered with treed fence lines. The sky is streaked with pink to indicate dawn, showing the hopefulness of a new day and reminding us that we will be with our Shepherd on that final New Day. Jesus faces the sheep and is attentive to them. In turn, the sheep are aware of His presence and are generally oriented toward Him, remaining relaxed, feeling free and confident to do what sheep do—sit, eat, and rest. Some of the sheep are closer to Jesus, some further away, but they (and we) are always well within His care.

Rebecca used watercolor paint, applying thin layers that build color and tone from lightest to darkest. The first step in creating this landscape painting was the sky with its soft wash of pink, blue, and yellow. The field and trees were painted next in several layers, followed by the shadows and details on the sheep and shepherd. Rebecca's cover art perfectly evokes the peace and calm found in the beloved imagery of Psalm 23, and her painting, like the content of this book, succeeds in drawing the reader's attention to Jesus, the Good Shepherd who promises to restore the souls of "the people of His pasture" (Psalm 95:7).

About Emmanuel Press

Emmanuel Press is owned by **REV. MICHAEL AND JANET FRESE**, who work together to develop ideas, edit and format manuscripts, and process orders in Fort Wayne, Indiana. Rev. Frese divides his time between responsibilities as Associate Pastor at Redeemer Lutheran Church, adjunct professor at Concordia Theological Seminary, and Wing Chaplain with the Indiana Air National Guard. In addition to her work with Emmanuel Press, Mrs. Frese spends most of her days homeschooling their three children, caring for their home and gardens, and planning family excursions to various historical sites in the United States and abroad. Travel has been an important part of the Freses' lives since the couple first met as college students during an archaeological dig in Israel in 1995. Later, the family lived in Germany for five years total, first for graduate studies and later with the military.

In 2004 Emmanuel Press was founded in order to publish *The Brotherhood Prayer Book*, a liturgical resource inspired by a German breviary and developed by Rev. Frese and Rev. Dr. Benjamin Mayes. Since then, Emmanuel Press has continued in its mission in making works essential to confessional Lutheran theology available worldwide. In addition to offering a host of classic reprinted books, including Paul H. D. Lang's *Ceremony and Celebration* and *What an Altar Guild Should Know*, Emmanuel Press has also published excellent, original devotional resources such as Rev. David Petersen's *Thy Kingdom Come* and *God With Us*, collections of sermons for Lent/Easter and Advent/Christmas.

Emmanuel Press seeks to collaborate with accomplished authors and translators to expand the variety of titles available to its customers. *Liber Hymnorum: The Latin Hymns of the*

Lutheran Church, edited and translated by Matthew Carver, was published in 2016, followed soon after by *The Great Works of God: The Mysteries of Christ in the Book of Exodus*, a collection of Christocentric meditations written by Valerius Herberger and translated by Mr. Carver. Both books have been well received and highly praised by a spectrum of theologians and parishioners. Also in 2016, Emmanuel Press released the first English translation of a collection of excerpts from Wilhelm Loehe, entitled *The Word Remains*, which features writings on the church year, the Word of God, and matters relating to the Christian life: faith, prayer, fellowship, worship, creation, and hope.

In 2017 Emmanuel Press partnered with Katie Schuermann to publish the second edition of *He Remembers the Barren*. In this revised and expanded edition, Mrs. Schuermann addresses questions frequently asked by those struggling with infertility, including the source of conception, family planning, and adoption, examining these topics through the lens of the theology of the cross and always pointing the reader to her identity in Christ. Readers often comment that Mrs. Schuermann's compassionate, honest insight into suffering and stress resonate with them, even beyond the subject of barrenness. Thus, revisiting an idea discussed with author Cheryl Swope several years earlier, Emmanuel Press considered how to broaden the discussion of suffering in the Church and invited a host of authors to contribute to Mrs. Schuermann's subsequent work, *He Restores My Soul*. In both of these projects, original artwork was commissioned for the covers, combining artistic beauty with rich Christian symbolism.

As well as publishing books, Emmanuel Press has produced a number of exclusive ecclesiastical greeting cards and Christmas cards. For more information and a complete listing of all items currently available, please visit www.emmanuelpress.us.

Acknowledgments

The chapters in this book are the natural yield of numerous seeds of wisdom planted by sage pastors, constant family members, and patient friends. If we have written something good and true, it is most definitely a gift "from above" (James 1:17) and should be credited to the faithfulness of all who have come before us. Thank you to our loved ones who daily bear our burdens "and so fulfill the law of Christ" (Galatians 6:2).

Specifically, we would like to thank Erin Maggard, Michelle, and many unnamed individuals for generously sharing their stories for the good of the reader. We would also like to thank Rev. Ron Stephens for the use of portions of his sermon for the third Sunday in Lent.

✠ Soli Deo Gloria ✠